My Secrets
of Playing Baseball

By Willie Mays

With Howard Liss

Photographs by David Sutton

New York The Viking Press

*To all of those great sports
enthusiasts who follow the games
- - especially my son Michael*

The editors wish to thank the San Francisco Baseball Club, Garry Schumacher, and the groundkeepers at Candlestick Park for their assistance. We also wish to thank Leo "Doc" Hughes, Miguel Murphy, and Eddie Logan for their help in this project.

First published in 1967 by The Viking Press, Inc.
625 Madison Avenue, New York, N.Y. 10022
Published simultaneously in Canada by
The Macmillan Company of Canada Limited
Library of Congress catalog card number: 67-13502
Printed in U.S.A.

All photographs in this book were taken by David Sutton
Planned and produced by the Sayre Ross Company, N.Y.
Designed by Jan Menting

Contents

Introduction

There are five hundred men who can play the game of baseball better than anybody else in the United States. They are the players who belong to the twenty major-league ball clubs.

But the only thing about those clubs that stays the same is the number, five hundred. Every year some players are moved out so that the new blood can come in. It happens to everybody, from the great ones like DiMaggio and Musial and Williams to the players who hang around maybe one or two seasons and then drop off. Someday it'll happen to me, much as I hate to think about it. On the average, four or five new men break in with a team every season, even when that team has won the World Series the year before. A club has to get new faces or it starts going downhill.

And that's the reason I'm writing this book—for the youngsters on the sandlots or in organized leagues, the high-school kids, who play pretty good baseball right now and have the same dream I once had, to break into the majors.

All the newcomers have one thing in common those first few days in the big leagues: they're scared! I remember the day I joined the New York Giants, a nineteen-year-old boy with a straw suitcase, and the firm conviction that I'd never be able to hit major-league pitching. Sure, I was hitting .477 when Leo Durocher sent for me, but that was with Minneapolis, then a Giants farm team. This was the big time, where the pitchers threw those good hooks and the blazing fast balls, and they had the control to knock the eyelash off a fly at 60 feet 6 inches. For a while it looked as if I had guessed right and Durocher guessed wrong. The first twelve times at bat I went hitless. Then came number 13, and I got my first hit. It was a home run into the upper deck, and against one of the best pitchers ever to come to the majors, Warren Spahn.

Nobody can stay in the majors without some help. I know dozens of people helped me, smart baseball men like Leo Durocher, Alvin Dark, Bill Rigney, Herman Franks, and many, many more. They took a young man with potential and showed him how to run the bases without bumping into every infielder on the other team; the fine points of hitting, fielding, throwing, running, sliding; even how to think ahead, figure the odds on a given play, and then, in the words of Casey Stengel, "how to execute what I learned."

I've been in the majors 16 seasons now, and I've played with or against some of the greatest baseball players in the history of the game: catchers like Yogi Berra and Roy Campanella; pitchers the likes of Whitey Ford,

Sandy Koufax, Juan Marichal, Warren Spahn; those solid infielders, such as Gil Hodges, Bobby Richardson, Pee Wee Reese, Ken Boyer; and the all-time outfielders, Williams, Musial, DiMaggio. I've watched them, studied how they executed fielding plays, how they guarded the plate, how they pitched, caught, ran the bases. I can honestly say that I learned something every day I went out to the ball park.

I'm going to cover a lot of the fundamentals in this book. Sure, I know, some of it may be old stuff for a few readers. But nobody knows everything about the game when he's first breaking in. The best ballplayer is the *complete* ballplayer, the man who knows everything about his position, and then learns just a little bit more. I know I'm still learning—every day, whether I'm playing or sitting on the bench.

A NOTE TO THE READER

This book has been designed to be read in two ways. First, there is the text, in which I discuss every part of baseball: fielding (position by position), batting, base-running, pitching and catching, strategy. Second, there are the pictures and captions, in which I have tried to demonstrate how I play the game.

So you may look at the text and pictures separately or together, whichever seems the best way for you to improve your own game, or—if you're strictly a fan—to understand and enjoy a ball game better.

1 Ballplayers

A baseball player is no different from any other athlete. Line up the boys who play baseball, football, basketball, hockey, soccer, and you'll find they all have the same things in common.

1. They're in great physical condition.
2. As a rule, they're fast of foot.
3. They have good coordination and timing. There's not a tanglefoot in the lot.
4. They all practice constantly.

Every one of those points leads into another. Let's take one example and see why I say this.

I've talked to athletes in every sport. They all say the same thing—the best all-around exercise in the book is running. Not walking, not jogging, not a medium trot. What I mean is the good, long, hard sprint.

You're playing in Yankee Stadium. You tag a pitch and send it over the center fielder's head. The Stadium has one of the deepest center fields in baseball, and a fast man has a chance to turn that hit into an inside-the-park home run.

Everybody knows that it's 90 feet between the bases; so the batter starts out running a 120-yard dash. Does it take stamina and good physical condition to run 120 yards at top speed? Try it yourself and see!

How much time does the runner have to circle the bases? Well, the track record for the 100-yard dash is something over 9 seconds, but that's without a heavy flannel baseball suit. And don't forget, this is 20 yards farther—at least! Some speedy guys, such as Maury Wills and Mickey Mantle in his prime, have been clocked in something like 12 or 13 seconds, give or take a few fractions. That's a lot of time for the outfielders to run down the

Overweight players can't get up speed. They can't stoop for a grounder, stretch for a wide one or pivot fast. Nobody can play baseball unless he's in top shape. It's hard work, but I always try to keep at it.

ball, pick it up, and start the relay going to the infield. And the man hasn't been born who can run faster than a thrown ball.

The run for the score has some built-in handicaps. This isn't a straightaway sprint for a finish line. The runner is going around in a circle, and every extra step he takes adds time to that big sprint. He's got to change direction fast, cut on a dime but stay balanced. It's pretty easy to get tangled up. The fast shift takes timing, coordination.

So how does this conditioned athlete, this fast young man, this coordinated kid learn to travel in a tight circle at top speed without missing a base or falling over his own feet? He practices. The manager and the coaches have him out there on the base paths, practicing the fast start and the fast turn until his tongue is hanging out.

Now let's take those requirements one at a time.

Good physical condition means strength in the muscles of the body. A batter needs power in his fingers, wrists, forearms and shoulders to whip the bat round. Ted Williams used to squeeze a rubber ball in each hand for hours at a time. That kind of strength enabled him to get a piece of the ball even when it was almost in the catcher's mitt!

Physical Condition

Whenever I see an overweight teen-ager, I get sore. Unless something's wrong medically, there's just no reason for today's youngsters to be fat and flabby.

Kids today are car-crazy. They hop into a set of wheels and go downtown to the pizzeria or the drugstore and stuff themselves with everything on the menu. Now, I'm not telling them to lay off the groceries. It takes energy just to grow up, and that comes from food. But the excess calories must be burned up, and the way to do that is *exercise*. That's what keeps the weight reasonable, gets the muscles toned up, takes the lard off the middle.

In my book—and most athletes agree with me—the best exercise of all is running. Boxers do roadwork all the time. In spring training, baseball play-

Almost every muscle in the body is used making a long throw. The muscles and tendons of the arms must be strong, yet loose and limber. The ankles and thighs have to be strong to take the shock of a fast pivot. The waistline has to be flat so the body can twist around. I never heard of any athlete hanging around the majors when he let his body get flabby!

ers start jogging and running around in the outfield to limber the legs, build the wind, condition the body all around. I think a teen-ager who lives less than a mile from school should keep off the bus and walk; better yet, let him run part of the way, and I mean run hard, as if he could hear the bell ringing for the first class. Going on an errand, he should run all the way to the store, and back too.

Most exercises are good. Bicycle riding is great for the legs, especially going uphill. Calisthenics, isometrics, gymnasium workouts, and just a little bit of weight-lifting keep the athlete in top condition. I don't recommend too much work with the bar bells because that tends to make a man muscle-bound, all tight around the biceps, shoulders, and chest.

There's no substitute for sports, winter and summer—swimming, hockey, track and field, even bowling, because that keeps the waist trim. When I was a teen-ager I loved to play basketball. All that sprinting, twisting, and turning is a great conditioner. I read somewhere that Mickey Mantle played basketball when he was in high school.

And don't short-change yourself on sleep. A doctor, a coach, or even the club trainer can tell you that the body rebuilds itself during sleep. Keeping late hours doesn't turn a boy into a man; it just turns him into a sleepy boy.

Another bad habit youngsters get into is smoking. I'm not being a wet blanket when I tell boys to lay off. Nobody needs Willie Mays to point out that smoking can be dangerous to health. It's right there on every package of cigarettes in clear print, and there was a report put out by the Surgeon-General of the United States that let loose with a lot of numbers and charts, all adding up to the same thing.

The same is true of drinking. Not only is it bad for the boy physically, but hitting the hard stuff can end up in tragedy. Some wise jokers get their

Getting the jump on the ball can turn many a "sure hit" into a loud out. The fielder has to start leaning the right way a split second after the batter connects and he can't make a mistake on the direction or distance of the hit. But even the best judgment won't help a bit without a fast start.

kicks tanking up on beer and then going for a drive. That's just dumb. There's an old gag about giving a drunk black coffee: he didn't become sober, he was just a wide-awake drunk!

Building Speed

Many coaches believe that any boy can attain some measure of speed. I agree. I've seen any number of youngsters who started out last-one-in-the-race and gradually worked up to respectable speed. That doesn't mean every boy can become a Bob Hayes or a Ralph Boston. Some talents the good Lord builds into a young man. But anybody's speed can be improved.

There are two kinds of speed a baseball player needs. One is the kind that helps a fielder catch up to the long fly ball over his head, or gets the base runner around the bags in record time. I call that "straight-away speed," even though the man may be running in a circle around the bases.

The second type of speed is the *fast start*. It's just as important as straight speed, maybe even more important.

One of the greatest outfielders in baseball was Joe DiMaggio. There were lots of guys faster than Big Joe, and he'd have eaten dust in a regular foot-race against them. But nobody I saw in my life ever got a faster jump on a batted ball. The hitter would tie into a pitch, send it booming out; DiMaggio would take one quick look and *zip*—he was off and running, making a bee-line for the spot where the ball would drop. Sure, Joe was an expert at judging a fly ball, but his quick start saved valuable time catching up to the ball. Baseball is a game of inches and split seconds.

It's the same with base running. The fast start helped Maury Wills steal over a hundred bases in one season. That boy takes off in high gear from a standing start. Maury's speed gives him a psychological advantage over pitchers. They all try to keep him from getting on base, because they know once he's on first, wham!—he's on second two pitches later. Pitchers try to work carefully on him, so carefully they end up either walking him or feeding him the kind of pitch he can punch through for a base hit.

Nobody's born knowing how to judge a fly ball. It means learning how to pick up the ball with the eye as it leaves the bat, judging its

Timing, Coordination

I don't think timing and coordination can be taught to a boy who hasn't got the raw materials. But most people do have them, and all that's needed is sharpening.

What is timing? What is coordination? Put it this way: they are part reflexes and part making the right move at the right time. The batter judging a pitch, stepping into it, bringing the bat around, and connecting solidly is using them. The infielder figuring the speed of a ground ball, moving his feet and arms and hands just right, and making the play with no wasted motion is using timing and coordination. *They are the way the brain and the body work together to get the job done.*

It's a funny thing about timing, coordination, reflex action: sometimes even the greatest athletes lose them all almost overnight. I remember what happened to Sugar Ray Robinson, one of the greatest pound-for-pound boxers who ever lived. When he started downhill it wasn't because he lost his punch; he could hit as hard as ever. But he said, "In the old days I'd see an opening and my right hand would leave my body without hardly thinking.

height, speed, direction, and distance, making allowance for the wind—then putting it all together, going back and making the catch.

All I needed was one fraction-of-a-second look. Later on, when I got older, I'd still see that opening, but it took longer. It was like my eye saw the hole in my opponent's guard, it sent a message through my brain and down to my fist. By the time I got ready to throw the punch, the opening wasn't there any more."

A baseball example of bad timing can turn up during a guessing game between a batter and a pitcher. The batter thinks, "He'll throw a fast one, so I'll start my swing right with his motion." But the pitcher crosses him up and throws a slow change-up. The batter swings, but he's way out in front of the ball. His timing is bad. He ends up looking foolish.

Practice

When I was a boy I read every sports magazine I could get my hands on. In one of them I read something by Don Hutson, a great pass receiver. Don said, "For every pass I caught in a game, I caught a thousand passes in practice."

When you get right down to it, there's no other way to learn. Physical condition, speed, timing, and coordination—none of these mean anything without practice. Spring training for major-leaguers isn't a vacation in a warm place when everybody up north is freezing. It's held so the players can sharpen up again after a long lay-off. Their muscles have forgotten what it's like to play ball.

Naturally, the best practice of all is playing baseball. That's when a boy lays it on the line—is he good, improving all the time, or just an average kid with a glove and spikes? Can the young outfielder judge the crazy dips and swoops a batted ball can take? Can he think fast when a play starts breaking and he's in the middle of it? Can he get at least one hit in a ball game? Does he throw to the wrong base, lose his head, just goof off?

One of the hardest parts of practice is the criticism a player takes from his coaches. Some players think a coach has it in for them when a flaw in style is pointed out. They think, "Aw, he's nuts, he's just tearing me down because he doesn't like me."

I know that when things start going sour for me—and all players fall into a slump at one time or another—I *beg* the batting coach to keep his eye on me, see what I'm suddenly doing wrong. Maybe I'm dropping my shoulder a little before I swing; maybe I'm striding too far; maybe I'm taking my eye off the ball. I can't see it, or I wouldn't be in the slump in the first place.

Practice can take all kinds of forms and can be done day or night. It doesn't take much light to go into the back yard and practice sliding into a base. Many times, during the winter, I go down into my basement and practice swinging a bat.

I've been talking about the basic requirements for any athlete in any sport. But I'm writing this book about baseball. Let's get started.

2 Defensive Baseball

In baseball, defense is more than 50 per cent of the game. The sluggers get the headlines, but it's the boys with the good gloves who make or break a team. I can remember one season when the New York Giants were banging the ball out of sight regularly, and they ended up with a club total of 221 home runs. They also finished in the second division. The pitching and the defense just didn't come through.

Look at the box scores to see what I mean. In most games, five or six runs are enough to win. In a lot of them the team on top does the job with some timely singles and doubles, and maybe one or two of the runs are unearned. A team doesn't have to score a whole lot of runs to keep winning consistently.

I'm not putting down the boys with the hot bats. My point is, any young man, with his eye on the majors, who thinks good hit, no field is enough to break into the big time is way off base. In fact it's just the other way around!

After all, how many major-leaguers hit .300? Perhaps fewer than a dozen in each league. But you take a man like Roy McMillan; he's the first one to admit he never broke down any fences with his bat, but he sure plays a lot of shortstop. Clete Boyer never hits for a high average, but plenty of clubs would like him to play third base for their side. He's made some game-saving stops you'd have to see with your own eyes to believe.

The Infield

The game of baseball is played mostly in the infield. Box scores show that maybe eight or nine put-outs per game are made by the outfield, so obviously the rest of them come via strikeouts, ground-outs, pop-ups, fouls, sacrifices, and so on.

In some ways the positions are played differently, and in other ways all the infielders must meet the same requirements. For my purposes, I can break the qualifications down into *team play* and *individual play*.

Team Play

All infielders must have good hands, and good throwing arms, and be able to move around like cats on a back fence.

They all field ground balls the same way: get in front of the grounder whenever at all possible, pick it up, and get rid of it fast.

When I first started using my "basket catch" some people acted like I'd invented something brand new. It isn't. In fact, this is the way a great many infielders latch on to a high pop fly hit in front of them. To my way of thinking, it works just as well for an outfielder.

I'm ready! I'm looking in toward the plate, concentrating on what's happening, so I can be off and running the instant the batter ties into the pitch. I'm leaning forward slightly so I won't be caught flat-footed; my feet are in position so that I can take off in any direction—in, out or to either side. The best advice I can give to any fielder is—just don't fall asleep out there!

When a rookie infielder gets a tryout, the coaches look to see if the kid plays the ball, or the ball plays the kid. A fielder can't wait for a ground ball to come to him; he's got to *move in on it,* because if he doesn't, a fast runner can get himself an infield single. It's very nice when a ball is hit to a fielder on a nice high bounce; baseball players says a grounder like that "has handles." But most ground balls don't behave to please infielders; they have top spin, back spin, they skid, swerve, slice, hook. There are all kinds of "English" on a batted ball. A good infielder doesn't waste time figuring out the bounce; he grabs it the fastest way, which is usually the best way. That's what's meant by playing the ball.

All the infielders have what I call "areas of responsibility." Each man is responsible for a special section of the diamond. When everybody is doing his job right, the whole team covers the whole infield for a given play.

Take the bunt defense, for example. When the pitcher serves the ball up to the plate, the whole team starts moving, even the outfielders.

The first and third basemen break toward the plate; the second baseman covers first base; the shortstop covers second base. (All the outfielders move in to pick up a possible wild throw.) But responsibility doesn't stop with movement. Once the ball is bunted, a play must be made, and it's the *catcher* who decides what that play will be. After all, he's the *only* infielder who has the play in front of him. He makes the call, and he does it loud and clear so there'll be no mistake. If he thinks there's a chance for a force on the runner going from first to second, he'll call out, "Second base!" and that's where the fielder should throw it.

Speaking of calling a play brings up the need for an "infield leader." Sometimes a pop fly is hit that can be handled by two infielders. Both have a shot at the catch and both want to make it. Somebody has to holler one of them away, or they'll knock heads. Most of the time the shortstop is the holler guy, although it can be somebody else. All infields should have one.

Another play that needs teamwork is the run-down, when a base runner is trapped between bases. Whenever possible there should be four infielders in on the play. One of those infielders has to be the pitcher, no matter where the base runner may be. Basically, the defense lines up like this:

If a runner is hung up between first and second, and he is the only base runner, the defense tries to pin him between the first and second basemen. Shortstop backs up second baseman, pitcher backs up first baseman.

If a runner is trapped between second and third, he should be pinned between the shortstop and third baseman. Second baseman backs up shortstop, pitcher backs up third baseman.

If a runner is hung up between third and home, third baseman and catcher pin the runner between them. Shortstop backs up third baseman, pitcher backs up catcher.

The pitcher, you see, is a kind of "roving defense man."

In making the run-down, the fielders should try to drive the runner back to the base he came from before making the throw. That way, if somebody misses a tag or the play is messed up, at least the runner doesn't advance and less damage is done on the error.

Now you might ask, "What happens when there are two men on base and one gets hung up. Where do the infielders go?"

Usually, when one runner is trapped, the other makes a break too, if only to take the pressure off his teammate. Sometimes the other runner *has to* move. If a runner is on second, and he sees his teammate trapped between first and second, he's got to do *something*. He can't just stand around with egg on his face.

So if the runner on second does break for third, that's where the play switches to.

The defense always goes for the front man.

And the fielders have to be alert, to know the difference between a real run and a bluff. The front base runner might just take a few steps toward the next base, hoping to draw a throw and take his teammate off the hook. An

Getting the ball back to the infield in a hurry is a combination of a lot of little things. Coming in to catch a fly, I've learned to try to grab it so that my left foot is slightly forward. That way I eliminate the need to take an extra step in order to get some power behind my throw. Try it yourself and you'll see how well it works out.

experienced fielder will bluff with him. He'll pretend to throw, just as the runner is pretending to run. And he'll keep an eye on the man he's got trapped. No sense in losing at least one chance for a put-out.

During a run-down it's almost a shooting offense for an infielder to leave a base unguarded. If a runner is trapped between first and second, the third baseman stays on third. He might be needed there if a throw got away completely and the runner tried to take one more base for good luck. Same thing with a catcher; he *never* leaves home plate, because that's the last base left to protect.

Infield Strategy

Infielders have to be on their toes every minute. They have to think ahead, figure a given play from all possible angles. That's especially true when there are runners on the bases. That's when the wheels start turning upstairs. "Suppose it's hit to me. Am I in position for the double play? Is this a double-steal situation? Will this guy at bat lay down a bunt? If he does, what will I do?"

Part of infield defensive strategy is in positioning. For instance, when a game gets into its last inning or so and the team in the field has a one-run edge, the first and third basemen will play close to the foul lines, much closer than they would normally play. Why? Because a ball that gets through along the lines usually means a two-base hit, while one that goes between first and second or between third and short is only a single. In a tight game it's better to have a runner on first than one on second base, in scoring position. It's the little things that count.

The number of outs and whether or not there are base runners figure in positioning too. There are three basic positions for the infield to take: (1) normal position, when there is nobody on base. The number of outs means nothing. (2) With less than two out and a runner on first, or runners on first and second, or bases loaded, the infielders move into double-play position. They are in closer than they would be in normal position. A ground ball takes less time to reach them, and they are a little closer to the bases. (3) With a runner on third base, and no chance for a double play, the infield will play in on the edge of the grass. This cuts down the possibility of a squeeze bunt. A runner can't advance on a ground ball that is fielded cleanly. If he does try, from that short range the runner is a dead duck. Any decent throw will beat him by a mile.

And, speaking of throwing, in tight situations sometimes it's a whole lot better *not* to throw the baseball at all. For instance, with that man on third and less than two out, if the batter hits a pop fly that an infielder gathers in on the edge of the outfield grass, it's possible the runner on third will bluff a run for home. A smart fielder, who has figured all the angles and thought ahead, knows good and well that the base runner isn't going any place. He's just hoping to draw a throw somewhere, and maybe it'll go wild. What the infielder should do then is hang on to the baseball and run it back into the middle of the infield. That way nobody is going to challenge his arm.

An infield that's sharp, looking everywhere, noticing everything, can save its club a lot of runs over the course of a season. Take the tag-up play. A batter hits a long fly that is caught, and the base runner tags up and advances after the catch. But sometimes the base runner gets a little overanxious, and he moves off the bag a fraction of a second before the outfielder makes the catch. If an infielder spots that, chances are the umpire does too. But the ump can't say anything; it has to be called to his attention by the infielder. That's what's called an "appeal play." So the infielder calls for the ball, steps on second base, and has a nice double play.

A similar play is made when a batter, running out an extra-base hit, fails to touch a base as he rounds it and heads for the next one. That too is an appeal play.

How to Play First Base

Ask me what a first baseman should look like, and I'll point to Willie McCovey, or to Joe Pepitone. Both are tall and have long legs and big arms and hands. Both are left-handed. There have been some good right-handed first basemen; Orlando Cepeda, who used to play with the Giants, is right-handed, and he plays the bag well enough. But right-handed first basemen are at a disadvantage, at least from a throwing standpoint. They have to shift their feet to make a throw across the diamond, while a lefty doesn't.

1. *Taking a Throw.* If a ground ball is hit to any other infielder, the first baseman makes a bee-line for the bag, turns, with his feet straddling first, and faces the fielder scooping up the ground ball. He *does not* go into his stretch until he sees where the throw is going.

Infielders rarely have time to get off a strike to first, particularly when the batter is fast. They want to get that throw to first. A first baseman gets used to all kinds of throws—high, low, to the sides. A good man with the glove can scoop the ball out of the dirt or climb way up there to pull one in that looks as if it's headed for the box seats.

If the throw is coming toward first but low, the first baseman touches the bag with his left foot and stretches *in* toward the ball.

If the throw is coming toward the outfield side of the base, he tags the bag with that same left foot and stretches *out* toward the ball.

If the throw is coming toward the home-plate side of the base, the first baseman shifts his feet, tags the bag with his right foot, and tries to catch the ball.

In some situations the first baseman doesn't do too much stretching. On a bunt, for instance, when the catcher pounces on the ball along the first-base line, the first baseman has to step out into the infield, touching the bag with his left foot, and giving the catcher a target to throw at. Otherwise the catcher's throw might hit the base runner.

Naturally, when a fielder's throw is way off target, the first baseman must forget about which foot tags the bag. He leaves the base and tries to grab the ball; better to let the runner reach first safely than to have the wild throw go right on through and give him an extra base.

2. *Throwing*. Actually, the first baseman throws the ball less than any other infielder. But when he does, it had better be a good one.

Most of the time a first baseman fielding a ground ball can make the play unassisted and beat the runner to the bag. There are times, though, when he gets one deep behind the bag, or when he has to go into the hole between first and second and can't regain his balance in time. That's when the pitcher is covering first.

The technique in throwing to a pitcher depends on a lot of factors. If the pitcher has been on his toes and has moved fast to cover the bag, the first baseman can lob the ball to him underhand. In a way the pitcher practically "runs into" the throw; the toss is made not to the bag itself, but to where the first baseman thinks the pitcher and ball will come together. It's thrown a little bit *ahead of* the running pitcher.

If the play is going to be close, one of those bang-bang types, the throw is harder and directly to the pitcher.

Either way it's a tricky play.

No matter what happens, though, the first baseman must keep his throw *away from* the area to which the runner is racing. If he messes up that throw, the runner is liable to plow right into the pitcher and knock him half-way into right field, and it'll be legal, because the base runner has the right of way. Better not to throw it at all than to risk a collision between runner and pitcher.

Another throw the first baseman is called on to make is the one that starts a 3–6–3 double play. This one is made sidearm, to avoid hitting the base runner moving to second base. Right after he gets off his throw, the

first baseman has to untrack himself, scoot back to first, and be in position to take the return throw from the shortstop. Again, the first baseman's throw is made to a specific spot, right over the bag, so that the shortstop can grab it, cross second, and return the ball for the DP.

3. *Holding a Runner Close To First.* When a runner reaches base, the first baseman moves over to guard him. He stands near the foul line, on the home-plate side of the bag, turned halfway to face the pitcher.

Making a tag on a pick-off attempt is an art. I used to get a kick out of watching big Gil Hodges make that play when Gil was with the Dodgers. It looked as if the pitcher's throw hit Gil's glove and the glove swatted the runner at the same time. The whole thing should be done in one smooth motion. It's not nearly so easy as it looks.

When the pitcher delivers to the plate, the first baseman moves back a few steps toward his normal position, so he can cover a little more territory. But he has to be careful about where he moves. If he should get in the runner's way and block him off from returning to the bag, the umpire can call interference.

When there are runners on first and second, the first baseman does not hold the runner close. He doesn't have to. But he still has to be alert for a different kind of pick-off throw, one from the catcher.

4. *Cut-off and Relay.* The first baseman is the most mobile of all the infielders when there are runners on the bases and the batter gets a single or an extra-base hit. When the wheels are turning, he has to be turning with

An outfielder should always try to be facing the infield when making the catch. If there are runners on, the fielder can see in a flash whether one of them is trying to move up a base. Notice, below, as soon as I've got the ball, my feet have automatically gone into position to make the throw. A fielder should do that whether there's a man on base or not. It's just a good habit to get into.

them. Let's take a situation where there are men on first and second (bases loaded would lead to the same movements) and see how an experienced first baseman moves around on various types of hits.

On a ball hit to left field for a single, he stays on first, just in case the batter takes too wide a turn. An unexpected throw might hang up the batter between bases.

On an obvious double to left, such as a shot ripped inside the third-base line, the first baseman moves to a spot between home, third, and the pitcher's mound. From that spot he can cut off the relay throw from the outfield and be in position to: (a) back up third base if the throw goes wild in that direction; (b) throw to second base if the runner takes too wide a turn; (c) throw to third if that runner takes too wide a turn.

On a single or extra-base hit to right field, the first baseman positions himself between first, home, and the pitcher's mound. He has the same options as he had when the ball was hit to left field, with one addition: since the second baseman will be covering the first-base area on singles to right, the first baseman might try a trap throw to first base if the runner there gets too careless.

Playing first is not complicated at all, not really. All the first baseman needs is three things going for him: good judgment, sharp eyes, and experience. If he's got the first two, the third one will come.

Second Base, Shortstop

Everybody connected with baseball talks about the importance of strength "up and middle," from catcher through the second-base combination and into center field. I don't disagree.

By far the most double plays in a game begin around second base, with either the shortstop or second baseman taking part, and very often both of them. I can't think of a pennant-winning club that didn't have an outstanding keystone combination. In fact that was part of the long success of the New York Yankees. Look at the list of great shortstops they came up with: Frankie Crosetti, Phil Rizzuto, Tony Kubek; and outstanding second basemen: Tony Lazzeri, Joe "Flash" Gordon, Jerry Coleman, and Bobby Richardson. Those guys turned the infield into a stone wall.

Good shortstops and second basemen come in all shapes and sizes. There have been some great little fellows, such as Phil Rizzuto and Nellie Fox, who played a lot of second base for the White Sox. On the other hand, Marty "Slats" Marion, who once played shortstop for the St. Louis Cardinals, was a six-foot-plus beanpole, and one of the best ever to come to the National League.

In some ways the shortstop and second baseman work the same way, and sometimes they act differently.

1. *Fielding and Throwing.* Most youngsters don't realize it, but the position of the *feet* is very important in fielding a ground ball. The left foot should be slightly ahead of the right foot.

You don't need a ball field to make the test for yourself. Stand with your legs spread slightly, a couple of feet apart, and with your *right* foot slightly ahead. Pretend to scoop up a grounder. Notice that you have to make a step with your left foot in order to throw. Now try the same thing with the *left* foot a little ahead. Notice that all you have to do is shift your *weight* to the right in order to throw.

That's a simplified test. Infielders don't stand still and let the ball come to them; they move in on it, or to the side. But it does show how little things save a step, a fraction of a second. That's what major-league coaches look for.

They also look carefully at what kind of throwing arm the prospect has. I don't mean that a kid has to have a rifle up his sleeve, although powerful arms never hurt any newcomer's chances. I mean they observe how fast the kid gets the ball away, how accurately he throws. A coach, if he has to choose between power and accuracy, goes for the bull's-eye arm every time.

Infielders should know how to throw the ball sidearm, overhand, or three-quarter motion. The sidearm throw is useful in two situations. When the fielder has to come in fast for a slow-hit grounder, he doesn't have time to straighten up and throw, so he heaves it across his body, practically on the run. And on a double play the sidearm motion moves the ball to first, away from the incoming runner, and reduces the chances of hitting him.

The overhand throw is made more by the shortstop than by the second baseman, and is generally made from the deep hole behind third base. That type of throw has the most power behind it. It also has the most chance of going wild.

The three-quarter motion, halfway between sidearm and overhand, is the most widely used and is most natural for the arm.

2. *Double Plays.* Between the time a double-play grounder is fielded and the relay man gets out of the way of the forced runner coming from first, there are three separate parts which must be combined into one smooth play in order for the DP to work. Any part that's flubbed breaks the whole thing apart.

The first part of the play is the throw to the pivot man. The type of throw depends on how much time there is and the distance to be thrown. If the batted ball was hit hard and fielded not too far from the bag, then the throw can be a "sure thing," an underhand lob to the pivot man, which reaches him somewhere between the belt buckle and the shoulders; chest-high is ideal. Other types of batted balls require faster throws made sidearm.

The important thing to remember is that the throw must go into the pivot man's path. Generally he is on the run, and if the toss is too far ahead of him he may not reach it; if it's too far behind him he must stop and reach back. Either way, the bad throw breaks up the double play and may even foul up the force-out. If ever timing and coordination were needed by a baseball player, this is one of those times.

The "tag and pivot" on second base is, without question, the trickiest piece of footwork in the whole sport. There are lots of ways to tag the bag and move away, and I'll run through a number of them. As to which one to choose, each player must use the one that suits him best.

(a) *Second-baseman pivots*

(1) The second baseman, running toward the bag, tags it with his left foot as he takes the throw. He takes another step with his right foot, bringing him over to the shortstop side of the base, plants that right foot firmly, and throws to first.

(2) Second baseman, running toward the bag, tags it with his right foot, then "pushes off" on that foot and throws to first, striding *into the diamond* to avoid the base runner. This has an advantage and a disadvantage; it saves an extra step and makes the play happen more quickly. But the second baseman has to have perfect control of his balance at all times, to be able to stop short, take the throw, pivot, and make his own throw. Another disadvantage lies in the fact that a base runner who gets to know the fielder's technique will make his slide in the direction of the second baseman's step, hoping to knock his feet out from under him and cause a bad relay throw. Base runners study *everything* about the enemy infielders if they want to get ahead in this business.

This is how most outfielders play a base hit. They get in front of the ball, kneel down and block it, to make sure it doesn't get through for extra bases. It's slower but it's also safer.

(3) Second baseman, running to the bag, steps over it with his left foot. He then makes a "hop-drag" motion; he hops across the bag onto his right foot, at the same time dragging his right toe across the base. Then he steps in toward the diamond, pushing off his right foot and onto his left foot and throwing. That's really taking an extra step, but it makes the throw more accurate, even if it does take extra time to make the play.

(b) *Shortstop pivots*

(1) Shortstop takes throw from second baseman as he lands on his left foot, just short of the bag. Continuing in stride, he tags the bag with his right foot, steps *outside* (the outfield side of the base) with his left foot, and throws.

(2) Shortstop takes the throw and hits the bag with his left foot. He steps back and outside, with a kind of "jump-hop" motion, coming down on his right foot. He steps forward and throws.

(3) Shortstop runs toward the base on the outside area. He steps over the bag with his left foot, hops to his right foot to throw, at the same time dragging his right toe across the bag.

The reason I don't play an outfield grounder that way is the waste of time. Look at the sixth picture. I'm down on one knee. I'll waste maybe a whole second getting up to throw.

These tag-and-pivot plays sound complicated. They *are* complicated. Many fans who watch a fast double play don't quite realize what a tricky maneuver they are seeing; they take it all for granted. Well, maybe they should. That's what ballplayers in the majors get paid to do.

The second baseman and the shortstop have to worry about different dangers where the base runner is concerned. For the most part, the second baseman has his back turned to the runner; he can't look around to see where the runner is because then he'd be taking his eye off the ball, which is the worst mistake a man can make in any sport. The runner can bang into him hard, like a football player making a blind-side block on a tackler. I've seen second basemen get badly banged up making the double play.

The shortstop can see the base runner all right, but his own momentum is carrying him right into the runner. At least the second baseman is trying to move away from the base runner. Therefore the shortstop has less time to get away safely after making the relay.

The third part of the double play is the throw to first base. *Don't hurry it too much!* I've seen experienced players get too anxious when they see that man pounding down the line toward first, and they draw back and let the ball fly. They don't plant their feet properly; they don't even look where they're throwing. It seems an awful waste of effort to go to all the trouble of getting a force-out at second and then throw the ball into the stands so that the other runner gets to second anyway.

Whenever possible, the throw to first should be made sidearm, to avoid hitting the base runner.

Speaking of double plays, there are maybe half a dozen ways the infield and outfield can pair up and knock off two outs. And that outfield-infield twin kill can be one of the prettiest sights in baseball.

I guess the one most common happens when a runner on third base tags up and tries to score on a fly ball. If the ball isn't too well hit, chances of throwing the runner out are good. If the outfielder is moving in on the fly, he's got forward momentum, plus a shorter distance to throw, and if the peg is on-target the fielder might get him. The most important element is the throw, and the most important part of the throw is accuracy. Not fire power; I mean right in the bullseye. The throw should be low, like a line drive, and it should reach the catcher on a bounce. I've seen guys with arms like rifles, and they put everything they've got into a throw without being sure where it'll end up. Throwers like that very often heave the ball into the stands!

Sometimes, when there are two or more runners on base and one out or less, an outfielder can come up with the D-P by throwing to another base— like maybe first. This is a tricky play and it might not work much of the time, but if it does, the fielder can kill off a rally real quick! Suppose there are men on first and third and one out. Batter hits a fly ball to medium right field. On such batted balls, almost always the runner on first moves off the bag a few paces, because there's always the chance the outfielder will drop it. It's possible—just possible, mind you—that a fast throw *behind the runner*, to first, might catch him napping and get there before he does. There can't be any hesitation on a play like that; the fielder has to size up the situation, make a decision and execute! And he'd better be sure the first baseman isn't caught napping, because the ball might end up in the dugout.

A double play can be accomplished by sheer perseverance. I saw it happen in a Dodgers-Yankees World Series. Johnny Podres was pitching. The Yanks got two on, nobody out, and the next man sliced a mean one down the left field line. It looked like a two-bagger sure. But the left fielder never quit on the ball; he kept running like a ghost was chasing him. He caught that ball on the run, whirled and fired back to the infield. The relay caught the runner trying to get back to first. The rally was dead and Podres went on to throw a shutout. If the fielder had played it safe, let up and conceded the hit, the Yanks would've won sure.

Sometimes, a center fielder in the right position, playing heads-up baseball, can turn an error into a double play. But he's got to be right there, on the spot, or it's no good. Say there's a man on first, it's a steal situation (I'll cover that later in the book) and the runner breaks for second on a three-ball, two-strike count. The catcher pegs to second—and the ball goes flying into center field. The runner would naturally take one look at the wild throw and make tracks for third. But suppose the center fielder was alert, and with the catcher's arm motion he started to move in fast, *just in case* of a bad throw. He's close enough to scoop up the ball and fire to third. And he's got a good chance to nail the runner. I've seen that play work a dozen times if I've seen it once. And even if there's no double play, if the runner sees the fielder come up with the ball, he won't take a chance on going to third, so at least there's an extra base eliminated.

A double play is teamwork, no matter who executes it. And unless each player knows how to work with every other player, you haven't got much of a ball club.

3. *Tagging a Sliding Runner.* The first thing to decide is, who makes the tag. No use in both men hanging around; one is enough.

As a rule, if a runner is trying to steal second, the shortstop covers the bag if a left-handed batter is at the plate; second baseman will cover if a righty is up.

If it's a case where the runner is going to second on his own batted ball, it depends on where the ball was hit as to who covers the bag. If the batter hits one to right or right center, then the second baseman will naturally run out to take the relay, so the shortstop covers. If the ball is hit the other way, the second baseman guards the bag.

There are two basic positions for the tagging infielder, and which one he uses depends on whether or not there's a man on third base.

With nobody on third, on an attempted steal, the fielder stands straddling the bag, behind it, turned to face the runner who is coming in. As the

It's harder for a right-handed outfielder to grab a ball hit to his right because he has to reach across his body to stab at it. But it's harder to throw the ball back

runner slides, the fielder leans down with the ball in his gloved hand and makes the tag, being careful to avoid the runner's spikes.

When there are runners on first and third, the fielder will stand in front of the bag at second. Should the runner on third break for home at the other end of a double steal, the fielder can throw the ball back to the catcher from a shortened distance.

The fielder has to be careful that the man on third doesn't bluff a throw out of him with a false start. Also, with the fielder in that position, it's possible for the runner coming from first to slide around him by hitting the dirt on the outside edge of second.

4. *Pick-off at Second.* Picking a runner off second is a pretty play to watch, from the defense's point of view. When it happens, they've taken a runner out of scoring position. But the poor joker who got nailed starts looking for a hole to crawl into.

A successful pick-off at second isn't like one made at first. There's nobody standing close to the runner holding him on, so he feels safe wandering a few feet off the bag. To make the play stick, a fielder has to get closer to the base than the runner is, and that is exactly the time the pitcher has to wheel and throw.

This play needs signals. They have to be given, and they have to be answered. Either the pitcher or the catcher gives the signals that the play

*to the infield fast when the hit
is to his left because then he's
off balance. On both kinds of
hits, the nearest infielder should
move out to take the relay throws.*

is coming up. If it's the catcher, he can take off his mask and adjust his cap; or he can do something with his glove that he doesn't ordinarily do. If the pitcher is giving the signal, maybe he'll toss the resin bag on the other side of the mound, or take out his handkerchief to wipe the inside of his cap. Anything at all.

The fielders show they've got the signal by kicking the dirt twice, by taking off the glove, by wiping their foreheads with the gloved hand. Once more, it can be anything at all that's been *prearranged*.

The pitcher goes into his stretch position, stops, and then he and the fielders behind him begin to count silently: one . . . two . . . three . . . four . . . *five!* At the final count an infielder breaks suddenly for second, as the pitcher whirls and lets fly.

There are all kinds of variations to this play. The fielders can make a couple of false starts before they decide to pull the pick-off. That gives the runner a false sense of security. He sees the bluff pulled a couple of times, he figures there won't be a throw, and he gets careless. Then, *wham!*, they lower the boom on him.

It's important that the play not be given away by an overanxious pitcher or fielder. The count should be made *silently!*

The bag is covered by the fielder who would normally cover it. A lefty at bat, shortstop covers. A righty at bat, second baseman covers.

The same type of play can be pulled by the catcher. He just calls for a pitchout, and the fielder breaks for the bag when the pitcher delivers the ball to the plate, because that is exactly when the runner is taking a few steps toward third. The fielder can pick up a couple of steps on the runner that way. The catcher throws through.

5. *Relays.* When a batted ball leaves the infield, the second-base combination starts moving. Where they move depends on how many men are on base.

With nobody on base, on an ordinary single to left, the second baseman covers second and the shortstop moves out into short left field. Chances are there won't be a relay, just a throw from the outfielder to the base. If the base hit goes in the other direction, the combination switches assignments.

With first base occupied, the chances are that the infielder going out into the short outfield may get a relay throw, depending on where the ball

was hit. On a long single into the alley, the runner on first may try to go around to third. A throw from the outfield may get him if the outfielder has an arm like Rocky Colavito's. But if the infielder does let the throw go through, there's a chance that the man who got the hit may try for second. It's strictly a judgment play. If the infielder cuts off the throw, he may be conceding third base to the runner, but he also has a better chance of holding the batter to a single, or, if the guy was sloppy in his running, hanging him up off first base.

With runners on first and second, a base hit brings other factors into play. Is the front runner a fast man, can he score on a routine single? Has the outfielder got a good arm? Is the team at bat too far behind to take risks, and do they have to play conservative baseball? I can show a few defensive maneuvers, but it should be obvious that the situation is too fluid to make a hard-and-fast rule. Sometimes, as a play starts to develop, even a well-drilled team has to play it by ear.

Most coaches tell me I play the ball as though I were an in-fielder, and maybe that's so, but it gets the job done. Follow the first sequence on these pages; observe that I'm moving in pretty fast. A few steps from the ball I start to lean down with my glove, because that's how I'm going to pick it up. Now turn the page and look at the rest of my pick-up motion.

(continued)

With men on first and second (or bases loaded), a single to left might find the second baseman covering second base and the shortstop, after a quick look into the outfield, moving over to cover third base (the third baseman moves to a spot between home, third, and the pitcher's box, to act as cut-off man).

A single to right sees the shortstop covering second, the second baseman covering first, and the first baseman acting as cut-off man (the reverse of the previous play).

On a long hit, such as a double down the line or between the fielders, or a triple over somebody's head, if the hit is to left, the shortstop runs into the outfield to act as relay man while the second baseman covers second. If a ball is hit the other way, the combination changes places.

Why do I say that sometimes a team has to make up the plays as it goes along? Because there are so many variables. The situation varies if there are men on first and third, men on second and third (nobody on first), with a

I'm almost in full stride when I reach down for the ball (and you've got to be in shape; a fatty can't stoop low on the run, that's for sure!). I grab the ball in my glove, and while I'm straightening up I transfer it to my throwing hand. I step forward and let it fly! This kind of move might be dangerous, because it's always possible to over-run the ball or drop it in trying to transfer it to the throwing hand. It takes practice!

bloop double that drops just beyond the reach of all fielders, with a solid line drive that goes out so fast nobody has a chance to move very far, et cetera, et cetera, et cetera. Every play happens just a little bit differently. That's what makes baseball such a great game.

Third Base

Most batters are right-handed. Most good right-handed batters can get around on a pitch and pull it down the third-base line. Sometimes, when we play a team with good right-handed hitters, such as Hank Aaron and Rico Carty of the Braves, I truly believe our third baseman is taking his life in his hands just showing up at the ball park.

1. *Fielding and Throwing.* A third baseman must have the reflexes of a tiger. Because he's so close to the batter, on a hard-hit ball he has only one fast shot at it; either he stops it, or he doesn't and it's by him. Many times he won't field the ball cleanly; it'll bounce off his chest or leg, maybe run up his

arm, hit him on the shoulder. Third basemen end up with more bruises than anybody else in the game. Old-timers say that Pepper Martin, who liked to block a grounder with his body, looked as if an artist had painted his whole torso with black and blue paint.

Except on slow grounders that he can reach by moving to the side, a third baseman doesn't do much running to his left or his right. Mostly he dives at the ball, and he'll trap it while he's sprawled out on the ground. Clete Boyer has that dive patented; I never saw anybody make such fantastic stops in my life. And, because so little time has elapsed between the hit and the stop, the third baseman can still get to his feet and throw out even a fast runner.

Mostly the third baseman throws either three-quarters or overhand, although on topped balls or bunts in his area he may have to throw sidearm or even underarm, because there's no time to straighten up.

On bunts with men on base, when the batter lays one down along the third-base line, the third baseman must make a quick judgment play. If the pitcher can reach it, the third baseman anchors on third and stretches to take the force-out throw. If he sees the pitcher can't get to it in time, he'll run in, scoop up, and make the play at first. On bunts the batter is trying to beat out for a hit, he has an even tougher play. Chances are he's been back behind the bag, and he's got a long way to go to reach the slow-rolling ball.

Pop-ups around the mound are generally the third baseman's responsibility, especially with men on base.

With a runner on second only, on a ground ball to the third baseman, he "looks" the runner back to the bag; then he throws. This is tricky, especially with a fast man at bat. In effect, the third baseman is bluffing the runner back to second without even taking a step in that direction, because that would take too much time. The fake throw is with the arm only. Then he wheels and throws to first.

The third baseman isn't used much on cut-off and relay plays. About the only time he gets into the act is described in the shortstop-second baseman section.

The Outfield

One October day in 1954, during the Cleveland Indians–New York Giants World Series, Vic Wertz came to bat with men on first and second. He tied into a pitch and boomed it out of there as if it were going into orbit. The center fielder turned with the crack of the bat and took off as if he were being chased by a hungry bear. About 460 feet from home plate the outfielder reached up and gathered in the shot like a football end catching a pass. He stopped and threw back to the infield. The runner on second tagged up and went to third. The runner on first was halfway to second, and he scooted back where he came from.

It's no big secret that I was the outfielder. It was a good catch, if I say so myself. But I had help.

I knew Wertz was having a hot day with the bat. I knew where he'd been hitting them, so I was able to play him, although nobody figured he'd hit that far.

Also, I've always been able to run pretty well. In addition, I had a fast start; I got a good jump on the ball. Those last two items spelled the difference between a long out and at least a triple for Vic Wertz.

Back in the days when he was a big winner with the Yankees, somebody asked Lefty Gomez if he had any special pitching secrets.

"Yep," Lefty said, grinning. "A fast outfield."

They say that Tris Speaker, maybe the greatest center fielder of all time, used to play a shallow center field because he was so fast and made such quick starts that it was next to impossible to belt one over his head. He saved hundreds of looping hits from dropping in for singles.

The same with Joe DiMaggio. He could judge a fly like a genius, and he got over in such a hurry he made even the tough ones look like routine flies.

Now, I don't think anybody can teach a man to judge a fly ball. In fact some of the best prospects can't make the majors because they have trouble in that respect. Back in the 1930s there was a ballplayer named Tom Winsett, who came up to the Dodgers with a big reputation as a slugger. He made good with the bat all right, knocking the paint off the Ebbets Field walls regularly. But he just could not get the hang of a fly ball, and he didn't stay up long.

Still, with enough practice, it can be done.

1. *Judging a Fly Ball.* In learning to judge a fly ball, several factors have to be considered: wind direction and velocity, and the type of ball park. Candlestick Park sometimes feels like a wind tunnel, and judging a fly there can be rugged.

The outfielder has to be able to pick up the ball with his eyes the moment it leaves the bat. That can be tough too, especially when there are no clouds in the sky. It's funny, but clouds help an outfielder see the ball; a straight blue sky can be murder.

Some fly balls are harder to catch than others. A line drive that's hit straight at the outfielder, maybe head-high, is one of the toughest of all. There's no way to judge how far the ball will carry, and hits like that tend to sail; they just seem to stay up there and refuse to drop.

These are some of the things an up-and-coming youngster has to watch out for in the outfield.

Part of the secret of getting under a fly ball is in the footwork. Very few balls are hit high and easy right to where the outfielder is standing. Most of the time he must run to make the catch: back, forward, to either side.

If the ball is hit over his head and to the right, the outfielder should make his first step with his right foot. If it's hit to his left, he steps off with his left foot.

Going back for a fly ball, a lot depends on which way the outfielder turns when he starts moving. If the hit is misjudged, if the fielder turns left when he should have turned right, he's going to get all tangled up, and lose sight of the hit. Get it right the first time!

Coming in for a fly ball is somewhat different. If the outfielder is coming in and to his left, his first step should be with the right foot. Why? Because he can get a longer stride and a faster pick-up into high gear that way. Try it yourself and see. When you are going in and to the right, the procedure is reversed.

One more thing about this business of judging flies: on those troublesome Texas leaguers, the kind of hit that seems too far back for the infield and too shallow for the outfield, the play should be made by the outfielder. The infielder, with his back to the play, has to grab the ball, stop, turn, and then throw. The outfielder is moving in, and he can just pick up the bounce and fire it in.

For the same reason, a ball that can be caught by either an infielder or an outfielder should be left to the outfielder. It's a lot easier to run in on the hit, keeping the ball in sight all the way, than it is to keep looking back over your shoulder trying to find the ball, the way an infielder must try to make that play.

2. *Catching a Fly Ball.* A lot of people have asked me about my "basket catch." I grab a fly ball with my palms cupped like a peach basket, down around my belt buckle. When sportswriters first saw me do it they thought I had invented a new way to field a ball, and some of them criticized me.

I always try to set myself facing squarely into the ball whenever it's at all possible. That way I'm in position to make the catch and return throw to the infield with no wasted motion. In baseball, like any other sport, it's always the split-seconds that count.

Actually, I didn't invent it at all. Some fellow I met in the Army mentioned it to me. I tried it, found it worked best for me, and that's how I catch fly balls. When "experts" told me I was doing it all wrong, my manager, Leo Durocher, growled, "He catches 'em, doesn't he? What more do you want?"

I bring up that story because there are a couple of ways to catch a fly ball, and each man does what's best for himself. By the way, the methods I mention work just the same for infielders as for outfielders.

When the fly ball reaches the fielder below the belt, the best way to catch it is to form the hands into a kind of basket, palms up, hands close together, the fingers pointing more or less in a downward direction.

When the ball is just about belt-high, about the same technique is used, except that the palms are cupped more and the fingers are pointing slightly upward.

When the ball is chest-level or higher, the hands are shifted so that the thumbs are together, fingers pointed up, palms slightly cupped.

Pop flies, especially those to infielders, can be caught by either of the methods described, whichever is most comfortable for the fielder.

Always try to get in front of the ball.

Whenever possible, use two hands for the catch. It takes less time to transfer the ball from gloved hand to throwing hand when both hands are on the ball to begin with. Simple enough?

A ball hit between the outfielders can cause all kinds of trouble unless the players know how to work with each other. Sometimes the fielders go into what the sportswriters call an "Alphonse and Gaston" act. "I got it," yells the center fielder. "No, I've got it," says the left fielder. "Okay, you take it," says the center fielder. "I thought it was your ball," says the left fielder. So what happens? While the outfielders are wondering who's going to make the catch, *nobody* takes it, the ball drops and rolls to the wall for a triple or maybe an inside-the-park home run. That's why the outfield needs a take-charge guy as much as the infield does. Usually it's the center fielder, because he's in on all balls hit up the alley.

On catchable fly balls, which both outfielders might be able to haul in, certain factors come into play. Are there men on base? Will a runner on third try to score, and is there a chance to nail him at the plate with a good throw? A split-second judgment must be made.

If the ball is hit into left center and the left fielder throws righty (that's usually the case), don't forget that he will be off balance. He'll have to stop,

An outfielder should try to keep his eyes on the ball from the second it hits the bat, until it's squeezed in the glove. Like they say, if you can't see it, you can't catch it! Sometimes, when the ball is hit over the fielder's head, he can't keep it in sight.

set and throw, or else make one of those fancy "whirl-around" throws, which are never too accurate. The center fielder is also off balance but not as much. It will take him less time to get the throw toward the infield. Besides, as I've mentioned, his arm is probably stronger anyway.

Even with nobody on base the two outfielders have to work together. One man should back up the other. In other words, if the center fielder sees that the left fielder is going to make the catch, he should move behind his teammate. First of all, that gets him out of the left fielder's way. Secondly, if the left fielder should accidentally drop the ball or misjudge it, the man backing him up is in position to pounce on the ball right away. It won't go all the way to the fence.

If an extra-base hit gets through, there's no sense in two outfielders chasing after it. One's enough. That would be the fielder closest to it. The other outfielder takes up a position to receive a throw and relay it back to the infield. That's teamwork between the outfielders.

There are two separate parts to a throw by an outfielder. The first part I call the "hop." The forward momentum of the body and the twisting at the waist take the fielder off the ground for a split second and bring him into position to get power behind the throw.

3. *Throwing.* All outfielders should throw overhand.

With runners on base, the catch and throw must be made with as little wasted motion as possible, and that requires a special technique all by itself.

The outfielder should try to move in on the fly and, if at all possible, catch it about shoulder-high, with the "thumbs together, fingers up" method. That way there is less motion needed to draw back the arm and let the ball fly. Of course, that's not always possible, and the outfielder has to make the best of his particular situation.

The outfielder, in making the throw, should make a sort of "hop forward," stepping a short step with his right foot, turning the body slightly to the right, planting the left foot, and firing in. This kind of movement gives him momentum; he can get his arm, shoulder, and body into the throw and execute a good follow-through.

4. *Ground Balls.* So far I guess I've stuck pretty close to the book. Maybe some experts might differ with the things I've said up to this point, but a lot of others would agree. However, when it comes to fielding ground balls, all the coaches and I part company.

Most coaches, and most books on baseball, tell the outfielder to make sure he gets in front of the ground ball to keep it from going through. Some even say to get down on one knee, to make sure.

I say, try to learn to scoop up the ball almost as an infielder would do it.

The feet should be planted firmly just before the throw is made, otherwise there won't be any zip behind the heave. The left foot strides forward and the fielder fires in. Outfielders must throw overhand. And the throw should be a line drive peg, not a high throw.

My dad (everybody called him "Kitty Kat") was an outfielder in the semi-pros, and he used to holler at me when I was a kid just starting to learn the outfield, "Pick it up! Pick it up! The ball won't bite you! Pick it up!" He was talking about grounders.

Looking at it logically, a ball that starts to bounce in the outfield has lost most of its steam. Even if it does roll past the outfielder, it won't go too far. An outfielder who can learn to rush in at top speed, bend low, and scoop that ball up quickly is going to make the difference between a batter stretching a hit into a double, and a batter either getting thrown out or staying put with a long single. Sure, a youngster who's just starting out may overrun the ball a few times while he's learning to make that play. But once he gets it down pat he'll be one up on the rest of the outfielders who can't execute that quick pick-up.

I've found that this method also gives me momentum to make a throw back to the infield. If that's different from what a young player's coach tells him, I'm sorry. I have to call the shots the way I see them.

5. *Working with the Infield.* On bunts, the outfielders run in fast to back up the bases in case of a wild peg. Right fielder moves toward first, center fielder behind second, left fielder toward third.

Outfielders back up infielders when there are men on base. On hits to left, while the left and center fielders are taking care of the batted ball, the right fielder will move toward first. On hits to right, the left fielder comes in.

In other words, all the outfielders act as possible back-up men, each behind the base closest to him.

An exception to this rule would be a long double in the left-field area. The right fielder, realizing there won't be a play at first base, moves closer to second, as the left and center fielders pursue the batted ball.

Errors

Every once in a while an infielder is going to bobble an easy ground ball. An outfielder is going to drop a simple pop fly. It happens. In the course of a season I make about seven errors. Sometimes nothing happens and we get the side out without a score. Sometimes I make an error that costs a couple of important runs. I've seen ball games where a good infielder messed up three straight ground balls, and on the last one he got so rattled he threw the ball into the stands. The crowd got on that poor kid so bad he wished he could dig a hole somewhere, crawl in and pull the cover over his head!

What advice can I give a young ball player who hits a bad streak and drops a few routine chances? None really. Except this: recover the ball fast and try to stop the runner from taking extra bases.

DON'T try to throw the ball just anywhere. Remember, a wild throw or a throw to the wrong base is worse than no throw at all. Pushing the panic button just makes things worse than they already are.

DON'T lose confidence in yourself because you booted a couple. There's nobody in the majors who hasn't messed them up a few times. I've seen my idol, Joe DiMaggio, let a baseball pop out of his glove now and then. Peewee Reese was such a great shortstop that the Dodgers bought the whole Louisville team just to make sure nobody else got him. Yet Peewee made more than a few errors in his great career, especially in his first couple of years in the National League.

And don't let up just because you're afraid you might make another error or two. I've seen some ball players who are more concerned about their fielding percentages than they are about trying to make the backhand stab of a grounder or an all-out attempt for the shoe-string catch. They just get *too careful!* But major league managers don't pay too much attention to averages. When they look over a young prospect they want to find out— is this kid AGGRESSIVE? Will he give every ball hit in his direction the old college try, will he hustle, will he climb that fence trying to spear that long high fly? Or will he quit when he thinks he can't make the catch, will he play it safe, will he go for a high fielding average instead of taking the risk that might cost him a couple of percentage points?

In short, the manager looking over the rookie is asking himself, "Is he the kind of fielder I want out there, when my team is holding a one-run lead in the ninth inning? Is he playing for the *team*—or for a lot of nice numbers at the end of the season?"

Hey, young ball player. Which kind of fielder would you rather have on *your* team?

3 Catching

Catchers call their gear "the tools of ignorance." I suppose that when it gets to be about 100 degrees out on the field, and the boys are weighted down with a mask, a chest protector, shin guards, and a heavy mitt, while they're constantly squatting down and getting up, running out to talk to the pitcher or backing up first, catchers think there *must be* an easier way to make a living. Add to that the constant threat of getting a mashed finger, a spiked foot, or the wind knocked out of them by a bulldozing runner trying to score, and maybe they've got a point to their thinking.

The catcher really controls the game. He calls for the pitches he wants, and 99 per cent of the time he gets what he calls for. The pitcher doesn't often shake off the catcher's sign, because he knows the catcher has his own private book on the hitters.

Catchers have the doggonest memories! Figure it out: there are 175 players in the league (besides their own teams), and they can remember

The correct way to receive a low pitch. Notice the position of the catcher's mitt, pointing down, so he can scoop it up. If the pitch was into the dirt he'd block it on his knees.

the strengths and weaknesses of most of the hitters; at least they know about the regulars. When I come to the plate, I can almost *see* the wheels turning in the catcher's head, and he's probably saying to himself, "Last time up Mays got a hit on a chest-high let-up pitch over the outside corner." And, buddy, you can be sure I won't see *that* pitch again for a long time!

Catchers need great legs. All that squatting and straightening up, maybe 125 or 150 times per game (that's about the average number of pitches thrown by a team's hurlers in nine innings), is hard on the calf and knee muscles. Catchers must be strong and durable, able to stand pain, because you *know* they're going to get hurt a few times during the season, from foul tips or wild throws or one thing or another.

In my time I've been fortunate to see some of the really great mitt men in action: Roy Campanella, Elston Howard, Yogi Berra. Just watching them operate is an education in itself.

1. *The Catcher's Stance.* The catcher has two basic positions: one is the position to give the signal; the other is the position to receive the pitch.

When giving the signal, the catcher is squatting down on his haunches, weight on the balls of his feet, legs spread comfortably, and mitt resting on his left knee, while his right hand flashes the finger signs.

When ready to receive the pitch, he crouches rather than squats. His legs are spread wider, with the left foot slightly ahead of the right foot. He

*The right way to take a high one.
Look close and you'll see the catcher
is on his toes, starting to rise up for
the ball. Catchers need a great sense
of balance, strong legs, quick reflexes.*

holds his mitt up as a target for the pitcher to shoot at. The bare hand, relaxed and maybe even slightly cupped, is held behind the thumb section of the mitt.

One mistake inexperienced catchers make is in the distance they stand from the batter. They're too far away, perhaps because they're afraid of getting hit by the bat. I'm not telling the green kids to get *that* close, but actually, within reason, the closer they stand to the batter, the better off they are. There's less chance of getting hit by a foul tip; it's a better position from which to throw the ball on attempted steals; it's a step shorter for a quick pounce into the diamond on bunts or topped balls; it makes it easier to catch the low pitches. I used to watch Yogi Berra play his position like the great catcher he was; it seemed that he almost moved in a few inches to catch the ball just after it crossed the plate area!

2. *Signals.* Signals should be uncomplicated and easy for the pitcher to read. Many times the catcher uses one finger to indicate he wants a curve ball, two fingers for a fast one, three fingers for a change-up, and so on. That's what he does when there's nobody on base.

All baseball players know about finger signals. Some have pretty sharp eyes, and they can see the catcher's fingers, especially when they're on second base, in a direct line through the pitcher and catcher. They can tip off the batter as to what's coming if they catch wise. That's when a little hocus-pocus is necessary.

Do you ever wonder what the pitcher and catcher talk about when they get into a huddle around the mound? One of the things they might discuss, with a man on second, is the *combination signal*. The catcher might say, "I'll give the signal three times. You only pay attention to the middle signal, forget about the other two."

So he returns to his position, squats, and shows one finger. He closes his fist. He shows three fingers. He closes his fist. He shows two fingers. The pitcher pays no attention to the first and the last signals. He remembers only the middle one. Three fingers; the catcher wants a change-up.

The catcher can vary this any way he likes. Or he can stop the action, call time, stroll out to the pitcher and change the whole thing around, so that the first signal is the one to pay attention to, or the third one. He can vary the combination signal, add numbers, until he runs out of combinations, and by that time the inning had better be over or the other team will have scored so many runs it won't make any difference which pitch he calls for.

3. *Making the Catch.* Catching the pitcher's throw is something like catching a line drive that might be dipping or curving, and the same technique is used. If a pitch comes in above the belt, the mitt should be held so that the fingers point up. If the ball comes in at belt level or lower, the mitt is held with the fingers pointing down.

Experienced catchers have a knack of "easing" a pitch into the strike zone if it goes a little off the mark. They don't use a fast jerky motion because that would give the trick away. I suppose sometimes it does fool the umpires; otherwise why would so many batters beef about called strikes? It doesn't always work, but it's sure worth a try. In this game of baseball, every little bit helps.

Pitches that bounce into the dirt must be blocked by the catcher's body or legs. It doesn't matter if the catcher doesn't make a fancy pick-up of the ball, just as long as he stops it and keeps it out in front of him.

Catching a foul can give a catcher a bad time. The toughest ones are those that go straight up over the plate. It's hard to pick up the ball at first, and to judge it properly. I remember one game when Allie Reynolds of the Yankees was working on a no-hitter. He had two out in the ninth inning, and Ted Williams came to bat. That's enough to give any battery a case of the jitters. Williams hit a foul pop-up a mile high along the first-base line. Yogi circled, got under it, got set—and dropped the ball. I think he wished for a gun so he could shoot himself. You never saw a sadder ballplayer in the whole world.

Fortunately, Williams hit another foul pop, right in the same place, on the very next pitch. Yogi squeezed that catch so hard he must have made the baseball lumpy.

Catchers gather in the pop-ups with the mitt held like a basket, the bare hand beside the gloved hand, both hands palm up. The instant the ball plops into the pocket of the mitt, the bare hand clamps down over it, to keep it from jumping out again.

In going after a foul pop, a catcher should rip off the mask right away, but he should *hold on to the mask* until he can see where the ball is and where it's heading. If he throws the mask away too fast, it's liable to land right in the path he'll take to reach the foul. Once the ball is spotted and judged, the mask can be tossed away in the *opposite* direction.

4. *Shifting and Throwing.* The only time catchers really have to worry about throwing, they also have to worry about shifting weight. It figures. Who cares how he throws it back to the pitcher when nobody is on? But when the runners reach the bases, every throw has importance.

When the ball comes over the plate or to the catcher's right, he is partially in position to throw already. The right foot is slightly back and the weight is on it during the crouch. All he has to do is step forward and throw.

When the ball is to the catcher's left, he is not in position to throw. What he must then do is give a short "hop," bringing the right foot back to the rear and turning his body slightly so that his left side is facing the pitcher. This gives him good throwing balance.

The peg itself is a "snap throw." The catcher brings his arm back just behind his head and lets fly overhand with a line-drive throw. There's a lot of wrist and forearm power in the catcher's throw to second base. He doesn't wind up; he doesn't use a full arm swing.

5. *Working with the Infield.* With nobody on base, a ground ball has the catcher running almost alongside the runner, outside the base line. He's hustling to back up a possible wild throw from the infielder. I've seen the catcher save an extra base on a bad peg many times.

On topped or bunted balls, the catcher flips his mask off and pounces. Whenever possible, he faces the first-base side of the diamond. That way the play is always in front of him, no matter where the base runners are.

One of the trickiest plays in working with the infield is trying to prevent the double steal. I touched on this play briefly when talking about the second-base combination, but I can go into it now in depth. I guess I know about double steals, because I've been in on quite a few of them in my time. I've learned to look at them from the catcher's point of view.

The double steal is worked most often with men on first and third and less than two out. It's a tough play to stop, but it can be stopped when the fielders have good arms. Basically, the idea is for the man on first to break for second. If the throw goes through, the man on third tries for home.

The catcher has no time to bluff a throw to either base. If he bluffs toward second and either looks or throws toward third, the runner there may not be going and the man coming from first will slide in safely. If he throws to second, and if the throw is even a little bit wild, the runner on third can make it in.

So the catcher takes a quick look at third to see where the runner is. He makes a quick judgment as to whether the runner has committed himself.

If he's staying close to third, the catcher pegs to second. As I noted in the section on shortstop and second baseman, the infielder there is in front of the bag. If he sees the runner on third try for home, he forgets about the man coming from first and fires back to the catcher.

Good arms can stop the play cold. Sloppy play can see a run score and a man on second base.

6. *Blocking the Plate.* Unless the catcher has the ball in his hand, he cannot legally block the runner from crossing the plate. To do so would be interference, and the run will score anyway. But once he has the ball, the catcher gets set for a head-to-head bumping with the base runner.

The catcher drops down on the base line in front of the plate, ball in his mitt, shin guards protecting him against the runner's spikes. The runner will make one of two moves: either he'll crash into the catcher, trying to knock him loose from the ball, or he'll try to slide around him and touch the plate with his hand or a reaching toe. The catcher must *not* allow the runner to slide under him. He's got to be down low enough so that there's just no opening for the runner. The tag is made with the mitt if the spikes are coming in, or with the firmly clutched ball if the runner is trying to slide around him.

7. *Which Pitch to Call.* Calling the right pitch isn't always a matter of the batter's weakness. I don't like to make any rules about catching and

pitching, because nothing in baseball is the same all the time. But in general, certain pitches should or should not be used, depending on the situation. I'll run down some of them and show why I say this.

In a sacrifice situation, when a pitch-out is impossible because of the ball-and-strike count, signal for a high fast ball, in tight. Keeping the pitch high may make the batter pop the ball into the air instead of laying it down. A fast ball, when it hits the bat, comes back to the fielder faster. Keeping the ball tight makes it hit the bat more toward the handle, so that there's a better chance of a foul ball instead of a good bunt.

In trying for a double play, call for a low curve, or a good sinker if the pitcher has one in his repertoire. The idea is to get the batter to hit it on the ground, and not give him a fast ball to jump into.

With the infield in and a runner on third, call for a curve. Once again, you want that ball hit on the ground, and a fast ball tends to "lift" when a batter hits it solidly.

With a fast runner at first and a steal suspected, stick with the fast balls. Even a change-up that will fool the hitter is no good. The runner, on a slow pitch, has a second more time to steal before the catcher has the ball in his mitt.

Don't feed bad hitters change-ups. Pitchers generally have trouble bringing the bat around. A good fast ball or a quick slider can blow right past the weak hitters before the bat is halfway swung.

In this sequence it's what doesn't show that counts! Notice, in the first frame, the catcher is crouched behind the plate as I swing. In the second frame he's starting to move. Where? He's actually right behind me, running toward first base to back up the first baseman. Somebody's got to be there in case an infielder throws wild to first.

Keep the ball on the outside for the good sluggers. That's a general rule, of course. Sometimes it's just as effective to jam them on the fists, so they only get some of the handle on the ball. But keep it away from the broad strike zone, neither high nor low.

With a man on first and a lefty batter up there, avoid the change-up. In such situations the first baseman is playing in to guard the runner, and on a slow pitch the batter can pull the ball right by him.

Don't be afraid to call for more than one pitch-out on a batter. If you call only one, the base runner gets to know your habits and has the pitcher and catcher at a disadvantage. Most base runners will not steal on the first pitch (on average), so the catcher can call for a normal fast ball or slider. But if a strike is called, the pitcher can afford to waste one or even two pitches on pitch-outs, looking to get the runner thrown out on a steal.

This shot was deliberately posed to show a catcher out of position. Can you see what's wrong? Look closely at the picture. I'm in sacrifice bunt position, meaning I squared away at the plate as soon as the pitcher started his delivery. The catcher had plenty of time to get set, yet he's still squatting on his haunches, weight far back on his legs. He should be in a crouch, with his weight forward, and ready to pounce on that ball as it hits my bat.

4 Pitching

Y ou'll notice that there are no pictures of me showing how to pitch. It's simple—I'm not a major-league pitcher and I don't pretend that I am. Can I throw a curve, a knuckler, a sinker? Sure! So can every ballplayer who's been around for a while. We often fool around in spring training or pregame practice with an assortment of pitches, because it's fun.

But we can't control those pitches. There's a big difference between a curve by Willie Mays and one by Juan Marichal, my teammate on the Giants. Juan's fast ball blows past the hitters; my high hard one wouldn't scare the weakest hitter in the league.

Besides, pitchers have to have special kinds of arms. Not the kind that can heave a ball from the outfield to the plate on one bounce, not the kind that can peg to second base on a snap throw, not the kind that guns one across the infield. Pitchers need arms that can throw and throw and throw. A 9-inning pitcher figures to make about 125 pitches per game, give or take a few. A relief pitcher has to have great control because there's a lot of pressure on him to get the side out.

I've been watching major-league pitchers for a long time. I kept my eyes open and asked a lot of questions. This is what I've learned about pitching in my years in the big leagues.

The one basic ingredient almost every successful pitcher must have is speed. If he can throw a good live fast ball he has a chance. Otherwise, forget it! Very few pitchers have made it into the majors without the blazer. Eddie Lopat of the Yankees was one; he had what the sportswriters called "three different speeds: slow, slower, and I'll be here next week." But Eddie Lopat was a rare bird.

Everything else can be taught, even control. When Sandy Koufax broke in he was so wild that many clubs turned him down cold. Leo Durocher is a good judge of potential in a ballplayer, but he watched Sandy throw a few pitches over the catcher's head, just shook his head, and walked away. It took Sandy a couple of years to learn where the plate was located.

I advise rookies to keep a couple of baseballs with them a good deal of the time—not to look at but to hold, grip, fool around with, to get used to holding one and feeling its seams. After all, the baseball is the most important part of the game, isn't it?

When it's been established that a boy has a good arm, the first thing he must learn is control. Without control he's just a guy with a fast ball and he won't last long. Way back years ago, the Dodgers had a young kid named Rex Barney, whose fast ball looked like an aspirin tablet when it came zinging up. He even pitched a no-hitter. But he was erratic, wild. Some days he'd get the ball over, and then nobody could touch him. Other days he'd walk himself right out of the ball game. The coaches tried everything; they changed his motion, shortened his stride, turned his body this way and that way. Nothing worked for very long, and finally he got so confused he couldn't throw at all and slipped out of baseball. Barney had all the equipment a young pitcher needs, speed, strength, and desire. But he couldn't master control the way Koufax did. Barney was an exception. Others have made the ball go where they wanted it to, after long and hard work.

Control also helps a pitcher stay around in the big leagues long after his fast ball has deserted him. Men such as Robin Roberts, Whitey Ford, and others have pitched good baseball past the age of thirty-five, when most pitchers are ready to call it a career. They have very little left in the way of consistent speed, but they have savvy and control. How does the pitcher achieve control? By practice, no other way. He listens to his coach, tries to follow instructions, and works to get the ball where he wants it.

Notice that I didn't say he gets it over the plate. A good pitcher *rarely* sends one right down the pipe. He works for corners and for different heights: over the outside corner, knee-high, or over the inside corner around the chest, or any kind of variation.

A pitcher has to have all the confidence in the world. He must believe that he can get them all out, that every man with a bat is his enemy and he's going to win the contest. Every game starts out as a no-hitter. Confidence makes the pitcher try to keep it that way, or to give up as few hits as he can. It isn't always easy when the pitcher sees a Ted Williams, a Joe DiMaggio, a Stan Musial swinging a bat. In his heart no pitcher expects to do too well with hitters of that stripe. Fortunately for the pitching profession, such hitters don't come around very often.

1. *The Warm-up.* Pitchers warm up for a very good reason, to limber up the arm muscles and tendons *slowly.* Any man, pitcher. or otherwise, who starts throwing the hard ones first crack out of the box will come up with a sore arm, I don't care who he is or what position he plays.

On a cool day it takes longer to warm up than on a hot day. About fifteen minutes are required when the temperature is on the chilly side. The pitcher should start with a few lobs, then work up to a medium-speed pitch; no curve, no change-up, just a nice throw. When the arm is warm and loose he can start the hard ones and the curves.

Only ten minutes are needed on a hot day, because the body is warm already. By the way, no matter how hot it gets, the pitcher should lay off the drinking fountain as much as possible. Too much water causes too much sweat, and too much sweat means loss of body salt, which weakens him. It's a good idea to take a couple of salt tablets during a game. Some people can't take them, though; it's just as effective to sit there with a salt shaker and lick some off the back of the hand between innings. It may not be proper etiquette, but the pitcher won't pass out from overexertion.

2. *The Wind-up.* Now we're set to start pitching.

Part of the wind-up—at least I consider it so—is standing on the mound and hiding the ball while taking the signal from the catcher. Some pitchers hold the ball in their gloves, others behind the leg, to hide it from the batter and the base-line coaches. The coaches, especially, are quick, smart birds. If the pitcher isn't hiding the ball too well, he may unconsciously tip off the pitch by moving his fingers to grip the ball in a certain way. Different pitches require different grips (I'll get to that later), and all coaches have enough experience to know the different grips.

With nobody on base the pitcher goes into the wind-up by starting a slight rocking motion. The right foot, which is on the pitching rubber, takes the body's weight as it swings forward, and the arms take a short downward swing in front of the body.

Then the arms start to swing up, and the weight is transferred smoothly to the rear left foot as the body leans back.

Now the pivot. The whole body, including the right foot and leg, on which the weight now rests, pivots in the direction of third base and the left leg, slightly bent, starts to kick forward, also in the direction of third base. The left leg should be kicked high, but not too high, as that sometimes destroys the balance. Then the left leg strides forward in the direction of the plate. The right arm starts to move into the delivery motion. Then the left leg hits the ground solidly, knee slightly bent to absorb some of the shock. The leg should be firmly planted *before* the pitch is actually made. Then the ball is released, just about at the point when the pitching hand is moving past the head but is not yet in front of the face.

Now, I've broken that down into great detail, and there might seem to be a lot to making the delivery. There is. But once the pitcher gets the hang of it, the whole thing becomes one smooth motion.

I've left the follow-through until now because it is important enough to have a separate paragraph. As the arm is extended and finished with the pitch, it keeps moving in the same direction it was going. The rest of the body comes around to follow the arm, and the pitcher ends up facing the batter, ready to field the ball if it comes his way.

Now let me point out that not everybody pitches according to the book. Take the leg-kick, for instance. I say don't kick it too high, and most pitchers don't. But Juan Marichal has a real high kick, one that brings the leg almost as high as his chest. The ball looks as if it's hidden until the time it leaves his hand. But Juan has remarkable balance and he can pitch that way comfortably.

One more point: I've described a right-handed pitcher's wind-up and throw. A southpaw simply reverses the arms and legs.

3. *Stretch Position.* With a runner on base the pitcher does not use a wind-up. He stands with the right side of his right foot against the front of the rubber. His arms go up or out, depending on his preference; then he brings them together at chest or belt level and *comes to a stop.*

That stop is important. The rule book says that the pitcher must come to a full stop in his motion for one full second in the stretch delivery, with his hands—and the ball—in front of his body. If he doesn't, it's a balk. Some crafty pitchers have cutie moves and they don't really come to the full stop. They get away with it somehow. But they're supposed to stop.

From the "set" position in which he stopped, the pitcher looks over his shoulder (right or left, depending on whether he's a southpaw or righty) to check the runner, then kicks and delivers.

4. *The Grips and the Pitches.* There are three basic deliveries a good major-league pitcher has: the fast ball, the curve, and the change-up. If he has those three down pat, he will do well. The other pitches—slider, knuckleball, screwball, sinker—can come later. A great pitcher like Whitey Ford didn't learn to throw the slider properly until he'd been with the Yanks for a number of years. He didn't have to; he was getting them out with just his three basic pitches.

But no matter what pitches a man has, none of them will do any good unless they're controlled. And even the big stars can have trouble on any given day. Some days, for reasons he can't understand himself, a pitcher's curve may not be breaking properly; it just hangs up there and the batter belts it frequently. Or he can't get the change-up over. When that happens, the catcher will find out the pitch that *is* working and stick with it most of the game. If none of the pitches is doing much, the hurler gets an early shower.

The important thing for the pitcher to remember in trying to fool the batter is that the curve and fast ball, which are used more than any other pitches in a game, must be delivered with the *same finger grip,* or the batter will be tipped off as to what's coming. For that reason also, all the pitches should come off the same pitching motion. *Don't* kick extra high for the fast ball, for example. That's like sending the batter a personal telegram.

The *fast ball* is gripped with the index and middle fingers across the seams and fairly close together and the ball of the thumb flush against the smooth side of the ball underneath it. The delivery has a kind of "buggy-whip" motion. The ball is held *firmly* but *not too tightly.* It should leave the hand straight off the fingertips.

The *curve* is held just about the same as the fast ball, except that the thumb grips the ball with its inside edge instead of the ball of the thumb. The arm and wrist rotate, to spin the ball, so that it leaves the hand across the index finger. Some people say that the ball does not really curve, that it's an optical illusion. Take it from a batter named Willie Mays, who has faced curves for a long time, they sure do break! The curve isn't thrown with as much speed as the fast ball. Properly thrown, it will start breaking about two-thirds of the way to the plate. A right-handed pitcher's curve moves away from a right-handed batter and into a lefty.

Most pitchers throw the *change-up* from "deep in the hand," that is, nestling against the long curve formed by the index finger and thumb. The fingertips overlap the ball and hold it fairly loosely. It isn't thrown as hard as the curve or fast ball. The most effective change-ups are those that are kept low. It's very tough to hit a slow pitch for distance because the batter must supply his own power. The faster a pitch comes in, the faster and farther it goes out when hit squarely.

Baseball players sometimes call the *slider* a "nickel curve." It doesn't have the speed of a fast ball and doesn't curve as much as a curve ball; it's somewhere in between the two. The delivery is also a compromise, partly off the fingertips and partly off the side of the index finger, with the same snap of the wrist as on a curve but faster than a curve is thrown.

The *screwball* is a reverse curve delivered with an entirely different action. Notice I didn't say different motion, because that would tip off the pitch. The wrist is snapped in the opposite direction, so that the elbow turns out and the ball slides off from across the inside of the middle finger. Thrown by a right-handed pitcher, the ball would break away from a lefty batter. Very few pitchers develop an effective screwball, even in the majors.

There are two types of *knuckleballs*. One is gripped with two fingertips on one seam, the thumb alongside one side of the ball, the ring finger and little finger holding the other side. This type is thrown with absolutely no spin at all. In the second type, the first two fingers are folded against the ball right on the first finger joints. When the pitch is released, the fingers sort of "flip" the ball and give it a slight downward spin. It's been said that no pitcher really knows where the knuckler is going or what it's going to do. It can dip, sail, swoop, curve, drop . . . I wouldn't be surprised if one of them suddenly backed up and flew back to the pitcher. Catchers and batters both get nervous when facing a knuckleball artist. With a man on third base the knuckler should not be thrown, for there's too much danger of a wild pitch or a passed ball.

The *sinker* used to be called the "drop ball" back in the old days. It's the same pitch. The sinker is an overhand delivery, snapped off across the top of the index finger. Otherwise it's like a curve ball.

There are all kinds of fancy pitches owned by a few pitchers here and there. The *forkball* is thrown from between the index and middle fingers and it has a peculiar motion, like "hipper-dipper zig-zag." It doesn't break very much and isn't a fast pitch. Mostly it's the novelty of it that might confuse a batter, and then only once or twice. The *palmball* is nothing but a variation on the change-up, with the ball delivered out of the entire hand, instead of just off the fingers.

Over the last few years there's been a lot of discussion about the so-called "spitball." Well, that doesn't have to be a ball moistened with saliva. Any wetness will do the trick; sweat, for example. And it really does work. A moistened pitch will do all kinds of tricks, and the pitcher is never sure what the trick will be.

Sometimes a pitcher gets hold of a ball with a "blemish," one that's been cut somewhere by getting hit by the bat or bouncing against a fence. Such balls are thrown out of the game, but sometimes a pitcher gets away with one or two pitches before it's discovered. It might be good to remember that such a ball always breaks away from the blemish. In other words, if the ball is pitched with the scar on the right side, the ball will break to the left, and vice versa.

5. *Fielding.* When a man like Bobby Shantz was pitching, his manager was sure he had five infielders on the diamond, not just four. Bobby was probably the best fielding pitcher ever to hit the majors. Many times he pulled himself out of jams because he was Johnny-on-the-spot with the glove.

In previous chapters I've covered most of what the pitcher's fielding duties are: help out on run-downs, back up various bases, et cetera. Other duties are almost too obvious to mention, but I like to keep the record straight.

On a play at the plate—any kind of play—the pitcher backs up the catcher. On a wild pitch or passed ball, when the catcher chases the ball, the pitcher covers home plate. On pop-ups around the plate, when the catcher and the first or third baseman have equal shots at the catch, the pitcher should call out the man to make the catch.

Mostly it's just a matter of common sense.

6. *The Pick-off.* From the set pitching position, the pitcher should be able to see the base runner simply by turning his head. If he has to turn his body too, he's not positioned on the rubber correctly. That goes for the runner on first or on second.

Before I go into the method of throwing, let's get together on this business of the balk, and what a pitcher is or is not permitted to do.

The rule book says that a pitcher does *not* have to come to the stop position in trying for a pick-off. He can suddenly whirl and throw as he's moving his arms down. He has to stop only when he's about to pitch to the batter.

The pitcher *must* step toward first when he throws from the set position. If he doesn't, it's a balk.

Once the pitcher makes a motion to throw to first he *must* go through with the throw. If he doesn't it's a balk.

The pitcher *is* permitted to bluff a throw toward second or third. He doesn't have to throw if he doesn't want to, to those bases.

The throw to first base should be made in one smooth wheel-and-throw motion. The throw should be a medium-speed fast ball, not too hard, not too easy. Some pitchers lob the ball to first a couple of times, to give the runner a sense of false security; then they burn it over to first. Sometimes this works, too.

A pick-off at second, as I mentioned previously, is made on signal. Otherwise the fielders are usually too far from the base to make the play work.

Pitchers have to watch the pick-off throws but not be afraid to use them to drive the runner back. No base runner ever stole on a catcher; he steals because the pitcher lets him get too big a lead.

7. *Pacing.* When a track star takes off on a mile run, he doesn't go all-out on the first lap, because he wouldn't be around at the finish. He saves something for the last kick. A pitcher should take the same attitude.

Pacing is a lot of little things. It's not working too fast, taking a short rest between pitches. Robin Roberts was a master of the between-pitches rest. He'd get the ball back from the catcher, adjust his cap, straighten his pants legs, hitch up his belt, move his shirt around, then look in for the catcher's sign. He probably used up a good ten or fifteen seconds just monkeying around with his uniform. Maybe that's one of the reasons he lasted so long in the majors. He knew how to pace his pitches.

Pacing is learning to vary the pitches successfully. Making every pitch the blazer takes it out of an arm. That's one of the reasons learning to vary the speed of a pitch is so important. Not only does it fool the batter, but it also takes some of the strain off the arm. You need less energy to throw a change-up than to throw a fast ball.

The better a pitcher is at pacing himself, the better his chance of getting the batter out. It's like a war of nerves. The batter is anxious to get up there and dig in, and the pitcher is just stalling around, taking his time, letting the hitter stew in his own juices. First thing you know the batter gets overanxious. He'll swing at almost anything. Then he becomes an automatic out.

5 Offensive Baseball

Good defense keeps the game close. But they still pay off on who has the most runs after the last out.

Babe Ruth revolutionized the game of baseball. Teams used to play for one run at a time, using a lot of bunting and stolen bases to get the marker up on the score board. The record books show how much baseball has changed. In 1918 Babe Ruth and Clarence Walker tied for home-run honors in the American League with 11 apiece, while Gavvy Cravath won in the National League with only 8 homers. Then the Babe started rolling, with 29 the next season, and then 54 and then 59. Well, pretty soon the other players got the message. Now every man big enough to reach the fences takes dead aim for them. I'm not saying that's good or bad, it's just the way things are. After hitting 500-odd home runs in my career, I'm certainly not going to put down the home-run fraternity. But I would like to point out one hidden fact to those who think muscles make great hitters: one of the greatest bat men ever to play professional baseball was Stan Musial, and he *never* won the home-run championship. Sure, Stan hit his share, and then some. But he didn't make it a habit to swing for the stands.

Batting

1. *The Bat.* That's the place to start offense, with the stick of lumber that makes the base hits. What kind should you use, how heavy, how long?

Until a couple of years ago, many players were using a light bat with a thin handle and a thick "business end." Such bats are easy to whip around fast, and when the hitter connects, the ball sails far and high. The trouble is, the heavy end of the bat had better hit the ball or it'll break off. A ball hit somewhere on the handle would either pop up or split the bat. Then some players started using a bat with a little more weight and a lot more handle. It was harder to swing around, but then the heavier bat made the ball fly just as far, and a ball hit off the fists had a chance to bloop out over the infield.

Maybe that's why I recommend an "average" kind of bat, sort of a compromise between the two kinds I've described. How heavy? How long? That's up to the individual batter, and it must suit *him*. No use trying to swing a Willie Mays bat or a Mickey Mantle bat if it doesn't feel right.

2. *The Grip.* In 1965 there was a lot of doubt that Mantle would do much playing. That guy was really hurting—bad legs, shoulder operation, all sorts of aches and pains. He found that he had particular difficulty getting around on the ball batting lefty (Mantle, as everyone knows, is a switch-hitter). So the great powerful slugger Mickey Mantle, who could bust a ball 450 feet with one swing—he *choked up* on the bat a couple of inches. Know what happened? He started banging the baseball right out of the park again! He swished the bat around faster, and with those huge shoulders and arms the

ball still rocketed out of there, even though he wasn't gripping the bat at the end while swinging left-handed.

I think there are too many players holding the bat down at the end who shouldn't be doing it, even in the majors. There's no shame in choking up a little. Bobby Richardson did it, Mantle chokes up batting lefty, and maybe half of the rest of the boys do it to varying degrees. I advise it especially when the pitcher has a good fast ball. It's easier to bring the bat around.

3. *The Stance.* I think I could do a whole book just about the different batting stances I've seen in the majors. Stan Musial stood up there with his feet fairly close together and body turned away from the pitcher. A sportswriter once described his stance as looking like "a man peeking around the corner to see if a streetcar was coming." Elston Howard stands with his feet spread extra wide apart. So did Joe DiMaggio. Gene Woodling, who used to play a lot of outfield with the Yankees, kept his feet together. A lot of batters stand so deep in the batter's box that the rear foot is practically outside the lines. They say it gives them a split-second longer look at the pitch.

I grip my bat down at the end, but that doesn't mean it's the right grip for everybody. Lots of major leaguers choke up a couple of inches. If you're able to get around quickly to hit a fast ball, okay, then hold the bat near the knob.

My stance. Look it over from the bottom up. Feet comfortably spread, weight evenly balanced. Knees slightly bent. Body erect, just a little bit bent over. Arms up and away from the body. This is an average stance, and it works best for most players. Some batters go into exaggerated crouches, and maybe it's right for them, but it's not for me.

Before and after the swing my hands are close together. Many inexperienced players grip the bat too hard. It's bad; makes the muscles tense up. Hold the bat firmly—not too loose, not too tight. Practice will help you get the feel of it.

The film strip on these two pages is a good example of my stance, stride, swing and follow-through. I've got my legs spread comfortably, feet set firmly, bat cocked, arms well away from my body. Timing the pitch, I begin to step into the ball and bring my bat around in a level swing. I've kept my eye on the ball all the way.

Other batters stand well in front inside the batter's box, so they can hit the curve before it breaks too much. Vic Power, who played for a number of teams in the majors, used to crouch real low at the plate. Yogi Berra stood straight up, erect. Some batters use a "closed" stance, with body turned away from the pitcher. Others use an "open" stance, so that they face the pitcher more.

The point is that each stance must suit the individual batter. Actually, there's no right way and wrong way to hit, unless the batter isn't getting any hits, in which case maybe the whole batting stance has to be changed.

Just as I recommend an "average" bat, I do the same for the stance. The young player should stand fairly well back in the batter's box, feet planted solidly about 18 to 24 inches apart, depending on which distance is most comfortable. The weight should be evenly distributed, body relaxed, shoulders loose, arms and elbows well away from the body. The bat should *not* rest on the shoulder; that tends to "tie up" the swing. It should be held back behind the body in a "ready" position.

4. *The Stride and Swing.* A good part of the power is a swing comes from wrist and forearm action. Maybe that's why Ted Williams used to keep small rubber balls in his hands all the time he wasn't playing ball. He would keep squeezing those rubber balls. He developed wrists and forearms that had all the power in the world, and he snapped that bat around as if it were a toothpick.

If my timing and swing are right, the fat part of the bat will meet the pitch slightly in front of the plate. Notice how I continue my follow-through after I've connected. Look closely and see that I've got myself a line drive over the infield. Man—I wish I could hit them all like that! I'd have a .350 average every year.

The swing has to be different, depending on where the ball is pitched. A ball around the knees requires a "semi-golf" swing, with wrist action whipping the bat down, around, and up. A pitch at the belt or chest level should have the batter swinging straight and even, as if he were hitting a line drive straight at the pitcher. Up higher, a pitched ball near the shoulders needs a "part chopping" motion. The bat's path should be *slightly* downward; otherwise the ball is liable to be popped up.

A lot of batters tend to overstride when stepping into the pitch. That throws the body out of balance. It's equally bad to stride too soon. The idea is to step into the pitch and have the bat meet the ball out in front of the plate, with the legs firmly planted for power.

Don't forget the follow-through. The body makes a complete turn as it follows the arms around.

On most occasions, the batter should hit the ball where it is pitched. Inside pitches can be pulled; a right-handed batter can get the bat around on an inside pitch and pull it toward left field. But very few batters have the power to pull an outside pitch, and that takes luck and great timing anyway. Outside pitches should be hit to the "opposite field," that is, a right-handed batter hits them to right field, a lefty hits them to left field.

A lot has been written about not trying to "kill the ball." I suppose that's partly true. Just as they say in golf, "Let the club do the work," a batter should rely on his bat to supply the punch. But I don't go along with that all the way, because it's a *wild* swing that will miss the ball, not a *hard* swing.

The batter has to put some gumption behind his swing, or the ball won't go very far. As long as the batter can keep his stride, balance, and swing under control, he can swing fairly hard at the ball and be sure to get a piece of it most of the time.

Sometimes a batter falls into a slump and he can't beg, borrow, or steal a base hit. There could be any number of reasons: he's striding too soon and too long, he's dropping his shoulder, his timing is off, he's uppercutting too much or chopping down too hard at the pitch, and so on. I've found that the best way to cure that is to try letting up on the swing and hitting the ball back to the pitcher. In other words, take a little of the power away and sort of meet the ball with an easy swing. I'm thrown out a good many times, but at least the rhythm and coordination come back, and pretty soon I've snapped out of it.

5. *Hitting behind the Runner.* It's a pleasure to watch a professional like Bobby Richardson, the former Yankee second baseman, when he's about to move that runner on first base around to third. Bobby hit behind the runner better than anybody else, for my money.

The basic idea is to put the ball into right field. For a lefty, that's his natural hitting area. Richardson is a righty, though. And he still does it.

The batter, as the pitch is delivered, shifts his weight slightly and steps back with the rear foot a couple of inches. Then, swinging a fraction of a second late, he just meets the ball with a short, sharp "punch" and bangs it to the right side of the playing field. If he's hit the ball properly, he's got a

looping liner to right field, on which the runner should be able to advance to third base. Even if he hits it on the ground, chances are he'll get the runner safely to second anyway, and maybe the ball will have "eyes" and roll through between the first and second basemen.

Hitting behind the runner is tricky, but don't forget, with a man on first base the baseman is guarding the runner, and there is more of a hole in the right side of the infield than there normally would be.

6. *The Bunt.* "For want of a nail a kingdom was lost," says the old adage. And for want of a good bunt many a ball game has been lost.

Look at how a bunt can pay off. Let's say it's a tight game, last inning, and the first batter gets a two-base hit. If the next batter can sacrifice him to third, any kind of medium fly ball scores the run.

Another situation: first batter gets on through a hit, walk, or error. A good bunt puts him in scoring position, where he can be picked up by a base hit of average depth.

But suppose the sacrifice fails? A valuable out has been given away; the team is worse off than before for that reason. And, if the runner is still on first, the possibility of a double play is still a threat to wipe out the rally. That little "drop dead" bunt can be a mighty powerful offensive weapon.

There are two kinds of bunts: one is used to sacrifice a runner ahead one base; the other is the "drag" bunt or "push" bunt that the batter is trying to beat out for a base hit. I'd have to say that Maury Wills is the best man

This is a good example of what I mean by a level swing. The bat comes around almost parallel with the ground. Too much up-swing and you get a pop-up. Hit down too much and you'll top the ball into the dirt. A level swing will get you a line drive.

The drag bunt depends on two things for success: bat control and a fast start. I slide my "top" hand up the bat handle, holding it loosely, and just let the ball meet the bat, giving it a little poke to make it move past the pitcher's box. In proper drag bunt stance (shown in this sequence), notice how I'm winging toward first with a running start!

in the majors at both types of bunts. Many times he even beats out the sacrifice bunts.

With the two different bunts there are two different techniques.

For a sacrifice bunt the batter squares around to face the pitcher as he goes into his delivery motion. The body is erect, the stance flat-footed. Why stand up straight? Because chances are the pitcher also knows the bunt is coming up, and he's going to keep the ball high. If the batter crouches, he has to bring the bat up, and he may very well pop into the air. The bat is held loosely in both hands, with the top hand sliding up the bat to a point just past the trade mark.

The best sacrifice bunt is one that hugs the foul line, and the best foul line is the one along first base. Of course that's not always possible, so the batter picks his spot and tries to drop the ball as close to that spot as he can. A good bunt will roll dead about a third of the way or halfway up the line.

It's important to control the direction of the drag bunt. If it's tapped back to the pitcher, that's a sure out. All the batter gets out of it is exercise. I always try to get the bunt by the pitcher, but to a spot where an infielder can't reach it in time to throw me out. Here the ball's dying on the edge of the infield grass. Man, take a look, that's a base hit!

Remember, the ball hits the bat, the bat doesn't take a poke at the ball. And, if you hold the bat loosely, the zip goes out of the hit and the ball rolls slowly toward the infielders.

On a drag or push bunt the batter does not square away, because that would tip off his intentions. He waits until the pitch has come about halfway to him. Then, leaning slightly toward first, he slides his top hand along the bat past the trademark and shoves the wood to meet the ball. Once more the bat is held loosely, but the batter shoves, pushes, or drags at the ball, with the tiniest bit of a poke he can manage.

Most of the time, especially when it's a lefty batter doing the bunting, the ball is aimed to go *past the pitcher* and toward the second baseman. For a left-handed batter the second baseman is playing deeper, he has a longer way to run in for the ball, and a speedster can beat the throw.

Right-handed batters can also drag one toward second base. Sometimes, however, they catch the third baseman playing a little too deep, and then a cute bunt along the line is very effective.

7. *Bad-Ball Hitters.* Young kids, just starting out to learn a little about baseball, are taught where the "strike zone" is—the area between the outside and inside corners, and between the knees and letters. I guess that's okay for kids, but for those more advanced, for whom I'm doing this book, that rule doesn't always hold up.

Yogi Berra was one of the best bad-ball hitters in the business. He'd swing at pitches around his ankles or even neck-high. And a good part of the time he'd come up with his base hit on those bad pitches. Sure, if he let them go by they'd be called balls. But Yogi figured he was up there to hit if he could, so he swung. I've gotten a lot of hits, even a few home runs, on pitches that were below the knees and maybe a little inside or a couple of inches outside.

My advice to a batter is, if you can reach the ball with the fat part of the bat and get some power into the hit, then as far as you're concerned it's a good pitch, whether it's in the strike zone or not. Learn which pitches you can and cannot reach.

The only part of a sacrifice bunt that really counts is making sure the ball hits the bat and rolls a short way out along the foul line in fair territory. All the batter is trying to do is move the base runner up a notch to the next base.

Base Running

One of the smartest pieces of base running I ever saw happened in the World Series between the Yankees and the Pittsburgh Pirates. The runner used his head instead of his legs and broke up a double play. That runner was Mr. Yankee himself, Mickey Mantle.

Mick was on first when the next batter hit a hard grounder to Rocky Nelson at first. Nelson must have figured that the ball was hit so hard Mickey wouldn't get far in his dash to second and would be tagged out easily. Besides, the ball was banged right over the bag while Nelson was practically standing on it. So he picked up the ball, stepped on first, retiring the batter, then turned to throw to second to get Mantle.

But Mickey didn't run very far. When he saw Nelson tag first he realized that he wasn't forced any longer; he could return to first if he could make it back. And that's just what Mantle did. He stopped short, dove back under Nelson's late tag, and got in safely. Quick thinking? Man, you know it!

Baseball players know the difference between a fast runner and a smart runner. Give me the second kind every time.

Notice my feet, body and bat positions. I'm squared away facing the pitcher, body erect, bat loosely held and parallel to the ground. Then I just stick the bat into the ball's path and top it into the ground so it rolls in fair territory.

Notice that my body is beginning to turn toward second base even before I hit first. I touch inside of the bag to cut down the distance I have to run. It's very important not to break stride. No matter which foot is used to tag first, the base runner has to avoid getting his feet tangled up when he pivots toward second. Rounding any base is trickier than it looks and requires practice. At right is a closeup of my feet rounding the bag. In this case it's first base, but the technique would be the same for second or third.

1. *Breaking from the Plate.* Early in the book I talked about the fast start. Nowhere is that more important than in chucking away the bat and starting the gallop to first.

If you have executed the follow-through part of batting, your weight should be on your front foot. So you dig down with that front foot, and the first step is made with the rear foot.

The rule in baseball is to keep your eye on the ball when you are batting, fielding, or backing up a play. This time, forget it. On a ground ball, get started fast and keep your eyes on first base. Never mind where the ball is; that's the responsibility of the first-base coach.

On every hit, run it out! If it's a hard shot between the infielders or a dinky dribbler back to the pitcher, *run it out!* The pitcher might slip and fall, or throw wild. The first baseman might drop the throw. These are human beings on the field, not machines, and they make errors even on the simplest plays. Hustle down the line! That extra step might make the difference between an out and an infield hit.

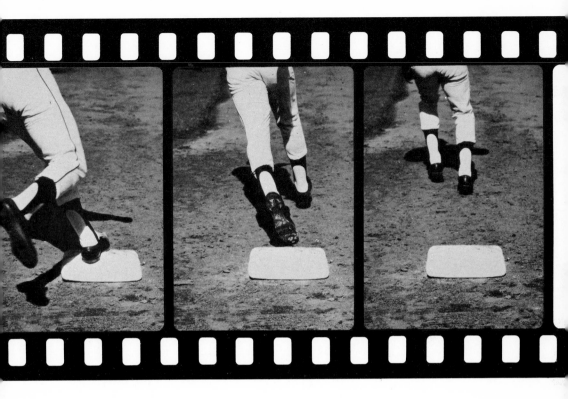

In that dash to first, make sure you stay away from the infield side of the base line. The path is wide enough—three feet—and to move to the far inside could result in a call of interference.

Most runners learn quickly to hit the bag in stride. A green kid might have to take a short step or two in order to make the base, because he has not learned to judge himself in running to first. After a while, though, it just seems to happen naturally that the last step is a normal stride step and hits the base.

After crossing first, the runner is permitted to run down the line a way to slow up and return to first (if he's got a hit).

On a base hit to the outfield, the runner should turn the corner and see about a possible extra base. He can keep his eye on the ball when it leaves the infield; in addition, the coach will keep him posted on his chances of stretching his hit.

On the outfield hit and turn, the question of "intent" comes up. The batter is in fair territory, and if he isn't going to second he must make that clear by slowing up within a couple of feet after turning first. Otherwise he may be tagged if the ball should be returned to first before he can get back safely.

2. *Rounding the Base.* On an extra-base hit, the runner begins his turn *before* he gets to first by moving slightly outside the base line. He leans his weight toward second, and touches first in stride, with his left foot if possible. He makes this slight outside turn and hits the inside of the base on second when stretching his hit to a triple, and on third when trying for home.

3. *Taking a Lead.* The technique is slightly different for a lead off each particular base. The runner has to take into account the positioning of the infielders, the type of pitcher on the mound, other possible base runners, and even the score at the time. Even the kind of batter at the plate can make a difference.

I'm often asked how long a lead a runner should take off first. That depends on the pitcher, how good a move he has to first, and whether he's a lefty or a righty. A southpaw goes into his stretch facing the runner. He doesn't have to look behind him; he sees every move the runner is making. Also, some pitchers, like Whitey Ford, have a deadly pick-off move. No runner can take a big lead on him and get away with it.

I can get back to first in about two big steps from the top of my lead. That's against a southpaw. I might go a little farther when a right-hander is on the mound. In edging off the base I keep my weight on the balls of my

feet, hands and arms loose and hanging, and I'm facing the pitcher. As he starts his delivery I take a couple of steps toward second, but if I don't intend to steal I move right back to first. The good catchers aren't afraid to throw, and a quick peg might catch me.

There are a couple of important don'ts in leading off first. Don't make fancy moves, like swaying the body from side to side. A pitcher's snap throw might catch you leaning the wrong way. Don't take your eyes off the pitcher, even for a second.

Taking a lead off second is different. There's no infielder to hold the runner close, and a catcher's pick-off throw has a lot farther to travel. Of course the runner can still get nailed by the silent-count play worked by the second-base combination. And since the throw to third is shorter than that to second, there is less chance of stealing third base. Put all these factors together and it comes out that the runner can take a slightly longer lead off second than off any other base.

He has to watch both infielders, sneaking quick looks back and forth to see their positions. When one of them bluffs toward the bag he has to be back, even when there's no throw.

The runner on third base takes his lead outside the base line, in foul territory. If a batted ball hits him, then it's just a foul, whereas if the ball hit him in fair ground he would be automatically out. Besides, he mustn't be in a position where he could interfere with a fielder's play.

If a pitcher keeps trying to pick me off first and I can get back to the bag too easy, then the lead I'm taking isn't long enough. If the play is close and I beat the throw by half a second, then it's just about right.

(continued)

Not many base runners steal home, so to some extent the pressure is off the pitcher. But there's always the chance of a wild pitch, a passed ball, or even a careless throw from the catcher that gets away from the pitcher.

In a try for a steal of home, it's best to attempt it when a right-handed batter is at the plate, because he tends partially to block the catcher's view of the runner. The batter is permitted to stay in the batter's box, which is another help to the base runner, because the catcher must move around him, and every extra step counts.

4. *Sliding.* Let me start this section with a type of sliding I think is dangerous: the head-first, hand-reaching-out bellywhopper. They say that Pepper Martin of the old St. Louis Cardinals Gas House Gang wouldn't think of sliding any other way. Good for him! Me, I'd rather go in feet first any time. It's a whole lot safer and gets the job done.

Sliding begins with the infielder. His position and where and how the ball reaches him help determine how the runner will slide. Another factor in sliding is whether the runner is stealing or trying to stretch a hit; or whether he is the front end of a double play. All these things will cause the runner to use either the *hook slide* or the *straight-in slide*.

The hook slide is designed to fool the infielder. It's as if you're giving him a piece of you to tag, and then you suddenly take it away from him.

The runner slides away from the direction the fielder is reaching for the ball. If the throw is coming from the outfield, the runner slides to the in-

I know that I tell young players to avoid the head-first slide, but going back to first base it's not so bad. I try to keep low and away from the first baseman, so he has to stretch to tag me. You can see I made it!

field side of the bag. If the peg is from the catcher, he slides around to the outfield side of second.

The slider leaves his feet and throws his weight in the direction he will slide. If he's sliding to the right, he throws his weight to the right. The right leg is thrown ahead and to the side of the base, while the left leg is dragged and hooks the base. The slide is begun as the slider leaves his feet off the tagging foot. In other words, if the slide is to the right, the runner takes off from his left leg, and that is also the leg that will catch the bag. All the action is reversed when sliding to the other side.

Some newcomers, just learning the hook slide, get overanxious. They put so much effort into it and slide so hard they go right past the bag. Or they get too cautious, and the slide falls short. It's just as bad to underslide as to overslide. Relax and let the momentum take over.

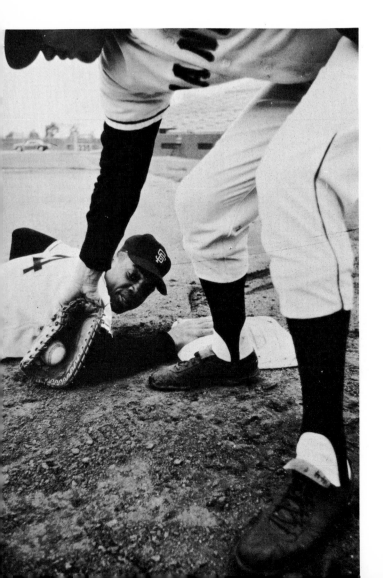

Nobody is getting fooled in the straight-in slide. (Some baseball men call this the bent-leg slide, because one of the knees is bent in going into the base.) It's used sometimes to break up a double play, and also when the runner has a throw beaten but wants to make sure he doesn't overrun the bag, and a slide is the easiest and best way to stop. The weight is thrown straight ahead, with one leg extended to make the tag of the base, the other leg bent under the extended leg's thigh, and the bent leg takes the shock of hitting the ground.

The bent leg has one more advantage: in case of an error on a throw, when there is a possibility of advancing one more base, it's easy to bounce up on the bent leg, as if it were, a spring, and take off again.

5. *Base Running in General.* Mostly, a good base runner just uses common sense. Some things nobody has to tell a ballplayer; he just sees the right way to do them.

For example, a base runner on second should hold up and not get anxious if the ball is hit ahead of him, to the shortstop. If he's forced, that's one thing; if he can stay put, let him stay put.

Taking a lead off first base, I set myself in position about one full length of my body, plus the length of my arms stretched out over my head. That figures out to something like eight feet, give or take a few inches. For me, that works out just about right, so I can manage to get back safe in case the pitcher pegs one over.

Or a runner moves halfway between bases on a fly ball, just on the off chance an outfielder might drop it. If it's caught, he trots back to first.

Or he makes sure he tags up and tries to score *after* a fly ball is caught, not a split second before.

Or he makes sure he touches all the bases as he circles them.

Or he tries for the plate from third when there is a runner on first and less than two out. Many times the defense tries for the double play. If the relay is late, you've scored. If they get you, there are still two men on base anyway.

Or he is smart enough not to interfere with an infielder making a play, even if he's right in the way.

Or a runner on first, when a ground ball is hit to the second baseman, who's in position to tag the runner and throw to first, should stop short and make the second baseman either chase him or throw to second. Don't just hand him a put-out; make the fielder earn it.

Or he watches the base runner ahead of him.

Or he pays attention to coaches and their signals.

Or—well, I said it before and I'll say it again. Baseball is a lot of little things.

6 Percentage Baseball

There's an old story they tell about Casey Stengel in the days when he was managing the Brooklyn Dodgers. It seems that Casey's club was losing by four runs in about the fifth inning, when Brooklyn got a rally started and filled the bases. Casey reached into his bench and came up with Babe Phelps, a catcher who could hit a ball into the East River when he connected. Phelps connected and tied up the game. But the Dodgers fell behind again, and in the ninth inning they got another rally started. This time poor Casey had no Phelps left to pinch-hit, and the man he did send up struck out.

"You stupid idiot!" a leather-lunged fan yelled at Casey. "Why didn't you save Phelps to pinch-hit in the ninth inning?"

I bring up this story in order to point out that baseball is a game of percentages. On average, right-handed hitters do a better job against left-handed pitchers. On average, a pitcher will bunt the ball with nobody out and a runner on first. On average, a base runner on second in a non-force-out situation won't try to go to third on a fast grounder to shortstop. Managers play the percentages. In the story about Casey Stengel, since he had the bases loaded he called on his best man, who delivered.

Baseball strategy begins with signals. A manager can't stop the action and tell each player what to do. He flashes the signs by way of the coaches, and he expects his players to know every signal cold. He also expects his players to catch every signal that's given. I've seen players get fined a couple of hundred dollars because they missed a signal and gummed up a play, even though that play might have had no bearing on the final score. The point is it *could have* meant the difference in another game, on a different play.

1. *Signals.* I guess everybody who ever watched a baseball game has seen signals given. The coaches don't try to hide them because they can't, and even if they could, they might hide them so well that the player they're intended for couldn't see them either. What they do is mask them, make the other team try to guess what they're doing.

For instance, let's say the signal to swing at the next pitch is touching the belt buckle and clapping the hands twice. The third-base coach, who relays the signal from the manager in the dugout, might hitch up his pants, stamp his feet, twist his cap, then touch his belt buckle, clap his hands, and keep right on going by wiping his fingers across his chest, kicking the dirt with his left foot, and so forth. The player at the plate, who has stepped out after each pitch to look at what the coach is doing, knows how to pick out the sign from all the rest of the fooling around. He'll obey and swing at the next pitch, unless it's aimed right at his body or it bounces into the dirt.

Clubs dream up signals for every possible situation, and situations they don't have signals for call for huddles between coach and player. That's why you'll sometimes see a short conference between the batter and the third-base coach; they're talking about something they don't trust to ordinary signals, such as "if the pitch comes in high, don't bunt, and if it comes into the strike zone, do bunt it."

The defense also has signals, as I pointed out in the double-steal and pick-off situations. The difference is that usually offensive signals do not require a reply signal, while defensive ones do.

2. *Special Situations.* Sometimes you'll hear players talk about a "steal situation." You might wonder how they know a player will try to steal at a particular time. It's not so hard to figure that percentage.

For example, suppose it's a tie game in the ninth inning. The first batter gets on base. The pitcher comes up next, and everybody in the ball park, including the peanut vendors, knows he'll try to bunt. So the pitcher bears down and strikes out the opposing pitcher.

Now the lead-off man is coming up. He doesn't hit for a high average, but he generally gets a piece of the ball, as most lead-off men do. He won't bunt, because there's already one out. He might get a base hit. He might also hit into a double play and kill the rally. This is a natural steal situation. The idea is to get the man into scoring position, so that if the lead-off man does get a hit, the runner may score. If there's a ground ball, the double-play danger is erased.

The pitcher knows it's a steal situation. So does the catcher. He may call for a pitch-out, either the first or second pitch. But he doesn't dare call for more than one, not in a late inning when a few unintentional balls added to the pitch-out could put the runner on second anyway, via a walk to the batter. See? The wheels are turning on both sides. They're playing percentages.

Another example: tie game, two out in the bottom of the ninth inning. The pitcher starts getting tagged and pretty soon the bases are loaded. A relief pitcher must be brought in. In the bullpen are two pitchers, a veteran knuckleball specialist and a young rookie with a good fast ball. Which man does the manager want in this situation? He starts figuring the percentages. The knuckleball pitcher might fool the batter with that dancing floater, but he also might throw it into the dirt. The catcher might not be able to handle one that goes real dipsy-doodle, and a passed ball would let the winning run in. On the other hand, the kid is green; this is a tough situation. Yet he might get that fast blazer over the plate on this one hitter. The players are tired that late in the game, and the batter might not get around too well on the fast pitch. See? Percentage baseball, figuring all the odds and making a move. Which relief man would *you* call?

Another situation: tie game, ninth inning. Man on third, man on second, one out, and a pretty weak hitter is at the plate. The infield is playing in to cut the run off at the plate.

The offensive manager thinks, "I need this player in the game for defensive purposes, so I can't pinch-hit for him, because if the pinch-hitter fails I'm worse off than before. But this batter probably won't connect for a long fly or drop in a base hit. I'll try the suicide squeeze; runner on third breaks for home with the pitch, runner on second breaks for third. If the batter can drop one down we win the game. If he misses the bunt my runner from third may be out, but I'll have the man on second moved to third and we'll still have one out left to us."

The trouble is, the defensive team has probably figured that out too. So the second the pitcher sees the man on third break for the plate he'll throw the ball high, maybe even try to hit the batter, because then the ball is dead and the runners have to go back to the bases they just left. Percentages.

Actually, this situation did happen in a ball game between the Yankees and the Indians. DiMaggio broke for home, and Scooter Rizzuto was at bat. The pitcher threw the ball right at Rizzuto, but he backed off, practically threw his bat at the ball, laid down a lovely bunt, and DiMag scored.

I could go on and on laying out different situations and showing how managers move and counter-move, but that would take about five more books, and I think the idea has come across.

Managers' strategy is often helped by gimmicks the players try, and, as all managers will tell you, every little bit helps.

For instance, when a batter is running out a triple, the shortstop may pretend to be waiting for the throw to put the tag on the man. Maybe he'll con the runner into sliding; it's happened before, that a fooled guy has slid into second base when he had a sure triple.

Or a batter may bluff a bunt, and when the infielders come charging in he chops into the ball, sending it through the hole just vacated by a fielder.

Sometimes a ballplayer overdoes things a little bit in this strategy game. They tell a story of John McGraw, the immortal manager of the old New York Giants. McGraw was a third baseman who figured all the angles. When there was a runner on third base, McGraw figured that any batted ball would start everybody scrambling, especially the umpires. In those days there weren't four umpires, as there are today, so the umpires had to do double duty. What McGraw did was grab hold of the runner's belt and hold him there for a while. The poor guy would scream blue murder, but McGraw made sure the umpires didn't see. One smart player caught on, though, and fixed John McGraw good. When the old firebrand reached for his belt, the runner quickly unbuckled it and took off, and there stood John McGraw, holding a man's belt in his hand while the runner scored.

7 Breaking into the Majors

No matter what city, town, or village I happen to be in, it's always the same old story, with fathers coming up to me and asking how they can get their sons into the majors. And I always tell them the same thing, that if their sons are any good and have played for any length of time, chances are they already have been spotted and tabbed for future offers.

Baseball organizations hire a great many scouts, most of them former major-leaguers themselves, to go from place to place in a particular area, usually around their own home towns, to look for new talent. Sometimes friends tip them off about a good prospect; other times it's just sheer legwork that turns up a budding star. Scouts can be found almost anywhere—at high-school and college games, or at games in the higher sponsored leagues, like the Babe Ruth League or the Kiwanis League. They even show up at sandlot games. Sid Gordon, who played with the Giants, was found at the Parade Grounds, near Brooklyn's Prospect Park. Harvey Kuenn and Sandy Koufax never played minor-league ball; they were signed right out of college.

And, if the scouts happen to slip up somehow, there are always tryout camps in spring training. On certain days during the regular season regular tryouts are held, and youngsters are invited to come to the big park and show their wares to the scouts and coaches.

The trick isn't getting anybody to notice the player. It's what happens to the kid later on that makes or breaks him.

What are coaches looking for? What do they hope to see in the prospect? Well, for sure it's the strong arm, the speed, the good swing, the sure hands. Those are *basic!* But they're also looking for a boy who has stability and good sense, who has a competitive spirit without the bad temper that sometimes goes with it.

They're looking for a young man who can adjust, who can pick himself up when something bad happens and start all over again. What can happen? Listen: Stan Musial started out as a pitcher, but he hurt his arm, and it was either get out of baseball or try another position. Stan didn't fight, he switched—and I know a hundred pitchers who wished he hadn't. Bucky Walters tried out as a third baseman, but he couldn't hit. So he switched to pitching and became one of the best ever to throw for the Cincinnati Reds. Sandy Koufax was a first baseman with the same story to tell.

And they're looking for boys who love the game of baseball. Sometimes, after I've played a twi-night doubleheader, and the club has to shower fast afterward and grab a plane to the next city in order to get there in time for another night game; sometimes, after day doubleheaders and make-up games, when I'm trying to grab a bite to eat and a little nap; sometimes, after a whole summer of this, I get to thinking, "Who needs this? I'm punishing my body to the limit, I'm not as young as I used to be." Sure, the pay is good. But there are some things money can't buy. Why do I do it?

I'll tell you why. Because baseball is my whole life. Right now it is, and probably for all the future I can see into. I think I can speak for all five hundred major-league players, and the kids waiting patiently in the wings for their turns at bat, and the veterans hanging on for just one more season. We love our jobs because they are fun. A guy like Mickey Mantle, who doesn't need the money or the fame, and who's had more aches and pains than a non-athlete will suffer in a lifetime, has operations and spends weeks in the hospital just so he can take one more swing at a baseball. He loves the game, and it has been good to him.

Have you got all those things going for you? Then come on in. Welcome to the club!

*Good Luck
to you all
Willie Mays*

I've played over 2,200 major-league ball games, but I still practice every chance I get. Any player who thinks his hitting, fielding, throwing and running can't be improved is on his way out of the majors even though he may not think so. We all have to practice.

WILLIE HOWARD MAYS, JR.
(Say-Hey)
(Willie's most common expression)

Born May 6, 1931, at Westfield, Ala.
Height, 5.11. Weight, 187. Brown eyes and black hair.
Throws and bats right-handed.
Single.
Hobbies—sports of all kinds.

Established following major-league records: most years, 150 or more games (13), 1966; most consecutive years, 150 or more games (13), 1966; most home runs, right-handed batter, lifetime (542), 1966.

Tied following major-league records: most years, 300 or more total bases (13), 1966; most consecutive years, 300 or more total bases (13), 1966; most home runs, six consecutive games (7), September 14 (2) and one each September 16-17-18-20-20, 1955; most games, three or more home runs, season (2), April 30 (4 home runs) and June 29, 1961 (3 home runs); most home runs, game (4), April 30, 1961.

Established following National League records: most home runs, one month (17), August 1965; most years, 100 or more runs (12), 1965; most consecutive years, 100 or more runs (12), 1965; most times, two or more home runs, game (54), 1965; highest slugging percentage, lifetime (.591), 1966; most home runs, lifetime (542), 1966; most years, 30 or more home runs (11), 1966.

First major-league player to hit 50 or more home runs and steal 20 or more bases in a season (51 home runs, 24 stolen bases), 1955; first National League player to hit 30 or more home runs and steal 30 or more bases in a season (36 home runs, 40 stolen bases), 1956.

Led National League in slugging percentage with .667 in 1954, .659 in 1955, .626 in 1957, .607 in 1964, and .645 in 1965; led league in total bases with 382 in 1955, 382 in 1962, and 360 in 1965; led league in stolen bases with 40 in 1956, 38 in 1957, 31 in 1958, and 27 in 1959; led league's outfielders in double plays with 9 in 1954, 8 in 1955, 6 in 1956, and 4 in 1965.

Hit four home runs in game, April 30, 1961; hit three home runs in game, June 29, 1961, and June 2, 1963.

Named National League Rookie of the Year by the Baseball Writers' Association and *The Sporting News*, 1951.

Named Major League Player of the Year by *The Sporting News*, 1954.

Named by *The Sporting News* as the Outstanding National League Player, 1954-65.

Named Most Valuable Player in the National League, 1954-65.

Named as Outfielder on *The Sporting News* All-Star Major League Teams, 1954-57-58-59-60.

Named as Outfielder on *The Sporting News* National League All-Star teams, 1961-62-63-64-65-66.

Received Gold Glove award as outstanding major-league fielder in center field, 1957; named for Gold Glove award as outstanding National League fielder in outfield, 1958-59-60-61-62-63-64-65-66.

Year Club	League	Pos.	G	AB	R	H	2B	3B	HR	RBI	BA	PO	A	E	FA
1950—Trenton	Int. St.	OF	81	306	50	108	20	8	4	55	.353	216	•17	5	.979
1951—Minneapolis	A. A.	OF	35	149	38	71	18	3	8	30	.477	94	5	1	.990
1951—New York	Nat.	OF	121	464	59	127	22	5	20	68	.274	353	12	9	.976
1952—New York†	Nat.	OF	34	127	17	30	2	4	4	23	.236	109	6	1	.991
1953—New York	Nat.				(In Military Service)										
1954—New York	Nat.	OF	151	565	119	195	33	*13	41	110	*.345	448	13	7	.985
1955—New York	Nat.	OF	152	580	123	185	18	•13	*51	127	.319	407	*23	8	.982
1956—New York	Nat.	OF	152	578	101	171	27	8	36	84	.296	415	14	9	.979
1957—New York	Nat.	OF	152	585	112	195	26	*20	35	97	.333	422	14	9	.980
1958—San Francisco	Nat.	OF	152	600	*121	208	33	11	29	96	.347	429	17	9	.980
1959—San Francisco	Nat.	OF	151	575	125	180	43	5	34	104	.313	353	6	6	.984
1960—San Francisco	Nat.	OF	153	595	107	*190	29	12	29	103	.319	392	12	8	.981
1961—San Francisco	Nat.	OF	154	572	*129	176	32	3	40	123	.308	385	7	8	.980
1962—San Francisco	Nat.	OF	162	621	130	189	36	5	*49	141	.304	*429	6	4	.991
1963—San Francisco	Nat.	OF	157	596	115	187	32	7	38	103	.314	397	7	8	.981
1964—San Francisco	Nat.	OF-1-3-S	157	578	121	171	21	9	*47	111	.296	376	12	6	.985
1965—San Francisco	Nat.	OF	157	558	118	177	21	3	*52	112	.317	337	13	6	.983
1966—San Francisco	Nat.	OF	152	552	99	159	29	4	37	103	.288	370	8	7	.982
Major League totals			2157	8146	1596	2540	404	122	542	1505	.312	5622	170	105	.982

† In Military Service most of season

WORLD SERIES RECORD

Year Club	League	Pos.	G	AB	R	H	2B	3B	HR	RBI	BA	PO	A	E	FA
1951—New York	Nat.	OF	6	22	1	4	0	0	0	1	.182	16	1	0	1.000
1954—New York	Nat.	OF	4	14	4	4	1	0	0	3	.286	10	0	0	1.000
1962—San Francisco	Nat.	OF	7	28	3	7	2	0	0	1	.250	19	0	0	1.000
World Series totals			17	64	8	15	3	0	0	5	.234	45	1	0	1.000

ALL-STAR GAME RECORD

Year League		Pos.	AB	R	H	2B	3B	HR	RBI	BA	PO	A	E	FA
1954—National		OF	2	1	1	0	0	0	0	.500	1	0	0	1.000
1955—National		OF	3	2	2	0	0	0	0	.667	3	0	0	1.000
1956—National		OF	3	2	1	0	0	1	2	.333	2	0	0	1.000
1957—National		OF	4	2	2	0	1	0	1	.500	2	0	0	1.000
1958—National		OF	4	2	1	0	0	0	0	.250	1	0	0	1.000
1959—National (both games)		OF	8	0	1	0	1	0	1	.125	5	0	0	1.000
1960—National (both games)		OF	8	2	6	1	1	1	1	.750	9	0	0	1.000
1961—National (both games)		OF	8	2	3	1	0	0	1	.375	4	0	0	1.000
1962—National (both games)		OF	5	0	2	0	0	0	0	.400	5	0	0	1.000
1963—National		OF	3	2	1	0	0	0	2	.333	1	0	0	1.000
1964—National		OF	3	1	0	0	0	0	0	.000	7	0	0	1.000
1965—National		OF	3	2	1	0	0	1	1	.333	3	0	0	1.000
1966—National		OF	4	1	1	0	0	0	0	.250	3	0	0	1.000
All-Star Game totals			58	19	22	2	3	3	9	.379	47	0	0	1.000

Courtesy of the 1967 Baseball Register, published by *The Sporting News,* St. Louis, Mo.